Introduction

When you've no money and dov... ,

Business transformation is a very difficult thing to start, let alone finish.

This is an amazing and mainly true story (except for Athena) of how a small business, with a defunct business model and in severe financial difficulty, fought to overcome insurmountable odds and huge obstacles.

Not just surviving, transforming. From a small network of reactive failing retail stores, into a cutting edge marking leading proactive business to business organisation, which has disrupted the industry.

What you'll read will shock you, amaze you and delight you.

Hopefully, you'll learn some stuff along the way too.

...buckle up and enjoy the ride.

Chapters:

1. 3 big bangs   3
2. Stranger things   8
3. Changing   12
4. Disruption begins   20
5. Operation business   34
6. Nearly fatal attraction   49
7. An unexpected thief   62
8. Bursting   70
9. The big move   78
10. Moving day   99
11. It's all about team   105
12. Predicting the future   121
13. Building   132
14. Finding our way   152
15. The unexpected   170
16. Simple Honest Service   191
17. The surprise   204

Chapter 1.   3 big bangs

Paul's head was in a mess, he had no idea what he was going to do. It was 6:30pm, he was sitting at a bar staring into a whisky glass, not wanting to go home to face his wife and children.

Paul's business was failing. He'd tried everything he knew, and still couldn't stop the decline.

Before the financial crisis business was booming, the company was profitable and growing. Since opening they'd gone from a single store, to four spread across East Lancashire.

Initially, what Paul offered was new and fresh. You couldn't get original printer cartridges from a local shop, let alone better value recycled ones!

At the time, there were no internet stores. Most people had to order printer cartridges from someone advertising in Computer Shopper, which took an age to arrive and were massively expensive.

When Paul opened the doors on his first store, the queues stretched far up the road. As the word spread, business rapidly increased; savings of up to 60% and fast great service was amazing people.

One store quickly turned into 2, then 3 and then 4. It seemed nothing could stop the company expanding. Except...

First came the recession, brought on by the financial crisis. Although it didn't have a massive effect on business, it did make people question where they spent their cash and it certainly slowed growth.

Then the real competition reared its ugly head; broadband had gotten much faster and affordable, paving the way for masses of internet shops, selling all sorts of stuff. Including printer cartridges.

Paul's business took a hit! Growth stopped completely. But two things halted a dramatic decline.

People liked the fact they were being environmentally friendly buying refilled cartridges. And. They could get their cartridges the very same day. Rather than having to wait for days if they bought on the internet.

The thing that really nailed it for Paul was something he didn't see coming.

Supermarkets had been around for years. But local councils made them locate way out of town on industrial or retail parks, so they wouldn't overly affect the small businesses in and around towns.

Shortly after, something changed though; Paul wasn't sure what. Councils suddenly started allowing supermarket chains to build massive stores within or right on the edge of towns.

You might think supermarkets only sell groceries. Not these bad boys; these sold clothes, household electricals, books, greeting cards, flowers. They even have butchers and bakers! Basically, the whole high street in one store.

And yes... They also sold printer cartridges.

Paul knew it wasn't just him who'd been affected. Just look at your own high street. Yes, some people point to internet shopping. But internet shopping at volume happened much later than the decline of our high streets.

Supermarkets started it and the internet is finishing them off.

Paul didn't see the breadth of products they sell as the main issue. Many products are more expensive than elsewhere. Take printer cartridges. They're much more expensive in a supermarket than from Paul.

Paul believes the issue is convenience. In modern society time is precious. After 6pm or on a Sunday is the time most people have available for household shopping. Supermarkets are open when most others are closed.

Years before, the man would go out to work, while the lady looked after the house and brought up the children. The high street was alive and local businesses thrived, as the ladies visited each day and bought fresh goods.

Most things change over time and this situation is no different. Some ladies didn't want to look after the house, they wanted careers (and rightly so). The economy changed too, and things got a lot more expensive, pushing both parents into work.

It's a very clever model. Build a big shop that sells everything in the middle of where people live and work. Then advertise the cheapest price for the most bought groceries (milk, eggs, bread) and open it 24 hours.

Time is so precious, when supermarket shopping, most people buy everything at the same time and don't even look or care about the price. They believe everything must be good value, because the essential items are.

It was devastating for Paul. Within 2 years he had multiple giant supermarkets within a mile of each of his stores. Even Paul's environmental model floundered, as the supermarket had a range of refilled cartridges supplied under their own brand too.

Paul's customers and revenue nosedived. It wasn't about service or price; customers continually rated the service as excellent, and prices were always a good deal cheaper than at the supermarkets.

People's lives had become much more hectic and their buying habits changed accordingly.

The supermarkets moved in for the kill, creating a marketplace where people could go when it was convenient and buy everything they required for the whole week.

Paul just couldn't see how the business would survive. Advertising and special offers just weren't working anymore- he had run out of options!

It wasn't as simple as just closing the doors. Paul was in deep. He'd literally bet the house, borrowing from the bank to fund their expansion. The situation seemed beyond repair and Paul was distraught.

They'd lose everything (including the house.) But his team weighed most on his mind. They relied on Paul.

Closing the business would spell great hardship for them and bring utter devastation for Paul...

Chapter 2. Stranger things

Paul raised his glass and admired the golden colour of the whisky, before taking another sip. He noticed a shadow appear to his right as he placed the glass down on the bar and set his eyes on an older lady with long flowing (nearly white) grey hair.

This lady appeared to be in her seventies and carried herself with such confidence, seeming regal. Her smile radiated warmth and her eyes were a deep compassionate blue. Dressed in loose fitting white robes, she glowed like a Greek Goddess.

Paul, unbeknownst to her identity or what to say, just stared in wonder.

"Hello, I'm Athena" said the lady with a warm smile, whilst moving her hand towards Paul.

Lightly shaking hands Paul said. "I'm Paul, nice to meet you."

Athena then looked straight into Paul's eyes saying softly; "I've been watching you and can't help notice you seem in real distress. I'm worried that you might be about to do something terrible."

Paul stared at Athena for what seemed hours, as tears formed in the corners of his eyes and rolled down his cheeks, landing with a splash on the polished oak of the bar. Athena immediately grabbed Paul and gave him a meaningful hug.

Paul hadn't experienced a hug like this since his mother hugged him on his first day at school. It meant something. Paul immediately felt safe and secure, his dark thoughts melting away the longer Athena held him.

After what seemed an eternity, they parted. Paul wiped the tears from his eyes, blurting; "How did you know I was in a dark place?"

"When you see someone looking into the bottom of a whisky glass, with the weight of the world on their shoulders. You can bet they're in a pretty dark place." Responded Athena.

"Now Paul, please tell me your story."

Paul had no idea who this lady was. But for the next hour he poured out his heart, telling Athena his story. Why they started the business. His hopes and dreams. The challenges they've faced and his devastation of the situation.

Athena listened intently, not interrupting Paul (except for the odd prompt or words of encouragement) until he'd finished.

Still glowing with that warm smile Athena said, "There is a way out of this Paul, but it's going to be one hell of a fight. It's going to take guts, sacrifice, determination and perseverance to succeed."

Paul stared into her deep blue eyes and said. "How can you be sure Athena? You've only just met me and learned my story. I'm at rock bottom!" he exclaimed, "the situation we're in is desperate and I just can't see how we can survive."

"Paul, I know we've only just met, and you don't know my skill set or understand how I may be able to help." Athena started. "But you must understand I have a unique set of skills, which have been honed over decades working with country and business leaders all over the world."

Athena continued, "These days I don't travel so much and can afford to pick and choose who I feel deserves my help. This isn't work for me and I don't expect any monetary gain. This is my vocation in life."

"I see and feel you're a good person Paul. You're honest, hardworking, you've got good virtues and your heart's in the right place. These are the things that you need to succeed. You just need a little help with strategy and direction."

"But why me and how do you know these things," Said Paul.

"I can't explain everything that happens," explained Athena. "All I can say is that wherever I am in the world I'm able to tap into people's feelings, simply by being close to them. Most people's values don't align with mine. But when they do and they desperately need help, I engage, like I'm doing with you."

"Wow!" exclaimed Paul. "You're an amazing woman Athena: a business angel even. I can't believe you've decided to help me. I'm all in. What do you need me to do?"

"It's not going to easy Paul. More like a war, with many battles to be fought along the way," Explained Athena. "I only have one rule though. When we meet and lay out the latest battle plans, you must carry out the orders we agree immediately and to the letter."

"Athena I'll do whatever it takes to make this business a success, I can't bear the thought of letting my team and family down. You have my word I'll carry out any orders we agree immediately and without question."

For the first time in a while, Paul latched onto a ladder of hope, with the determination to make it to the top, no matter how hard the climb.

Chapter 3.   Changing

The following day Paul and Athena met for their first battle plan session: at Athena's home.

Athena's house was a palace, huge marble columns, inlaid with gold, held up the porch to the front entrance, an abode fitting of a goddess.

Athena led Paul into her study, filled with books, which reminded Paul of those decadent ancient libraries of the past or on-screen.

On the meeting table, in the centre of the room, was a steaming pot of fresh coffee and some freshly baked shortbread biscuits. They must have been freshly baked, as they smelled divine.

Athena motioned for Paul to sit down. "Paul, before we start, I've got to be honest and clear with you. What we're about to do will take years to implement. During which you'll be tested to your limits and taken to some very dark places. I need to be sure you understand this and you're all in."

"Athena you've given me an opportunity to save my team and family from a disaster, which was also going to consume me too," said Paul. "What you're doing is truly amazing. What I said yesterday about you being my business angel is the truth, and I'll do whatever it takes to turn this situation around."

"Okay Paul," Athena said. "It's time we started and there's no going back."

"Today, what we need to decide is the future, what your industry is going to look like in another 10 years Paul and then work backwards," started Athena.

"From what you've already told me and the way I see it, there's no future in providing your services in the way you currently do to only consumers."

"I agree," Said Paul. "Whichever direction we take, we've got to repackage our offering and remove our total reliance on consumer business."

"Yes, that makes sense," agreed Athena. "You certainly need to build some services that will appeal to business too. But it's not about providing the exact same solutions as your competitors either. To stand out in the market you've got to cause disruption, either through new products or in the way that your current products are delivered."

Athena continued. "Listen Paul. A couple of things are clear; you are honest and transparent, and you deliver world class service to your customers. We can take these virtues and package them into the new services we develop, which will enable us to really disrupt the office technology industry."

"Don't get me wrong, it's going to take years and we'll need to change and build things slowly over time, as and when they're affordable to do. But I really think you have a great opportunity to create something unique."

This gave Paul a rush of excitement; he beamed at Athena. "But I'm still not sure what's going to happen in our industry over the next 10 years, making it impossible to see the direction we should take."

"Exactly why I'm here Paul. Don't worry," Athena explained. "During the last 10 years I've worked with the CEO's of HP and IBM on business strategy. If I could pick one industry where I'm right up to speed with current and future developments, it's office technology."

"That's amazing," said Paul, dazzled. "You're truly a business angel Athena. Working with HP and IBM must have provided some real industry insights. But we're little tadpoles to these giant whales. How will strategies built to deliver services to national and global organisations help us?"

"This is how we're going to gain a critical advantage Paul," Athena said with a wink.

"You see. At the enterprise level where IBM and HP operate, their overriding strategy is to be the number one provider of technology services to large organisations."

"To enable this, they develop solutions to cater for every technology need with these types of organisations. Things like; telecommunications, computing, print technology, cloud services, business systems and software. And then wrap them into a package to suit each individual customer, which is headed by a program manager and invoiced for monthly."

"What I'm proposing Paul is quite radical. I see. 10 years from now. Small and medium organisations will be open to such services too. Subscription services will become the norm."

"Take TV; In the UK you already pay a license to watch the BBC or a monthly fee for SKY TV. These are subscriptions. In the future internet broadcasters will appear too, offering many types of video on demand type subscription packages."

"How do you know all this stuff?" Said Paul, who was clearly mesmerised.

"Like I said yesterday Paul. For decades, I've worked all over the world with some very intelligent people. Strategy is the thing I live for and sharing it with people like you, brings joy to my heart."

Athena continued. "We're going to take this enterprise strategy, repackage it and deliver it to small and medium organisations in a subscription package. It'll take time. But we'll release each element as we build them."

"What a strategy Athena. I love it and really believe we can achieve it. What about. 'To make office technology solutions affordable for all'. As our vision statement."

"Perfect," Athena smiled.

"Where to start though..." mumbled Paul.

"At the beginning Paul," stated Athena. We've got to stablise the decline in your consumer business quickly. Otherwise they'll be no cash to fund our plans, let alone pay salaries."

"What do you suggest then?"

"Whatever we do has to move us towards the overall vision. To keep doing the status quo is not an option," Athena said. "At the enterprise level they provide a complete print technology solution, including the hardware, cartridges and maintenance, which is paid as part of their monthly charge."

"Why can't we do something on a smaller scale for consumers?" The biggest issue as you've already identified, is convenience. So, why don't we design a service which is more convenient than consumers buying printer cartridges online or from the supermarket. Whilst also saving them some money."

"What if we can design a home printing solution, where consumers don't have to buy the hardware, the cartridges or even buy replacement printers when they break. Letting consumers print as much as they want without worrying about the price, with cartridges sent to them for free on demand."

"Bloody hell Athena! That sounds like a winning formula. And I'm assuming consumers would sign up to a monthly subscription?" asked Paul.

"Exactly," Countered Athena. "That's enough for today Paul. When we meet again in 2 weeks, I want you to present me with a fully costed home printing solution, together with a suggested monthly subscription price, based on the average use and cost of cartridges for a typical family with children."

The following day Paul pulled his team together and went through the strategy set out with Athena the previous day. The team seemed visibly excited and committed to help and support Paul in the times ahead.

Paul's team had vast experience in printer technology and knew he'd be stupid if he didn't ask them to get involved. Keen to help, they all immediately agreed to meet at Paul's house on Saturday to brainstorm.

It was an interesting session and didn't start the way Paul had envisaged. What surprised him, was the negativity in his senior team, those who had been with him for 10 years or more.

Don opened by saying; "look Paul, I know we need to change some things. But I can't really see our customers being willing to sign up to a monthly subscription." Which led to Harry chipping in too. "Yeah, I agree with Don. I know my customers and not many will agree to something like this."

Paul was a little shocked and knew immediately he had an enormous challenge to change the mindset of his own team, before he could even think about disrupting the consumer printer technology industry.

"Look," said Paul. "I know you've all had a few days to think about Athena and the new consumer strategy. And I've no doubt you're all unsure and a little scared about changing our business model."

"Especially not knowing how our customers are going to react. One thing I can assure you though, is if we don't give this new consumer strategy a shot. It won't be long before the business folds and we all lose our jobs."

Paul then recited a well-known Albert Einstein quote to his team. Saying; "Einstein's definition of insanity was doing the same thing, repeatedly, but expecting different results." "This is exactly what we've been doing."

Don then said, "I understand Paul. I think I can speak for the whole team on this. Clearly, we must do something different. But we're scared. Change is daunting for all of us. And just the thought of asking customers to sign up to a monthly payment plan is terrifying."

Warmly smiling at his team Paul said confidently. "You've got to trust me. We're going to build a product so great and compelling that customers are going to ask to be signed up, and even recommend us to all their family and friends too. This is the start of something very special."

They spent the next 4 hours working out which printer technology to use based on quality and cost of cartridges, mapping out supply chains, working out cost models and setting monthly and annual subscription fees based on business margin requirements. The office hummed like a war-room.

Paul spent the following days crunching data and analyzing customer trends.

The target market for their new home-based print technology service was families with school children, home workers and the self-employed. As these have the biggest technology need and will receive the biggest savings.

What Paul had to work out was on average, how much these people were spending on printing activities on an annual basis. And what their biggest issues were with their current printer technology setup. No easy task.

The results were quite astounding. On average this demographic buys a set of printer cartridges four times a year and replace their printer every three years. What was also very interesting. In the main, they bought original cartridges, usually from the supermarket, whilst doing their weekly shop.

Doing the Math, Paul quickly worked out that this demographic was spending on average around £280 a year on cartridges and replacement printers. To disrupt the industry and gain traction Paul had to half this.

Chapter 4.   Disruption begins

Two weeks passed in what seemed a blink of an eye. Paul was stood once again outside Athena's Greek mini palace, admiring the alabaster columns.

The large oak door swung open startling Paul. Athena stood before him wearing a warm smile, looking every bit as regal and goddess like, as Paul had remembered.

"Hurry Paul come in we've got loads of things to get through today." Athena said excitedly. "I've been looking forward to meeting again all week. I'm bursting to know what you've found out and how things have developed."

Athena quickly led Paul into the study, the smell of fresh coffee and shortbread biscuits hung in the air. They both sat down at the meeting table. Paul poured them a coffee and offered Athena a biscuit.

"It's been a strange couple of weeks Athena." Paul began. "I left our first meeting invigorated and so motivated to kick start some real change."

"I thought it was important to get the team engaged and asked if they'd attend a brainstorming session at my house on the Saturday."

"They seemed really keen to help and all attended. But it didn't get off to the greatest start. They really pushed back against what we're trying to achieve. Saying no way would customers buy into a subscription service."

Athena prompted Paul; "What did you say to them Paul?"

"Well." Paul continued. "I said. I've no doubt you're unsure and a little scared about changing our business model. Especially not knowing how our customers are going to react. But one thing I can assure you. If we don't give this new consumer strategy a shot, we're dead in the water."

"What did they say to that Paul?" Athena asked.

"Don seemed to be the team's nominated spokesperson," said Paul. "He said, clearly Paul, we must do something different. But we're scared. Change is daunting for all of us and the thought of asking customers to sign up to a monthly plan is terrifying."

"Change is difficult Paul." Athena said softly. "Most people are scared to death of change and would much rather carry on doing the status quo, even if it's not working anymore. How did you leave it with them?"

"I asked them to trust me and said we're going to build a product so great and compelling customers are going to ask to be signed up, even recommending their friends and family too. And that it's the start of something very special." Replied Paul.

"Great reply Paul," said Athena. "Did it have the desired effect?"

"It seemed to," Paul countered. "We spent the next 4 hours brainstorming printer technology, supply chains, costs models and subscription fees. Coming up with some fantastic formulas, solutions and ideas."

"Well done," smiled Athena. "It's important the team is 100% behind us. Believe me, they'll have many more wobbles along the way. Our job is to lead from the front, reassure them and pick them up when they're down."

"Back in the early 90's IBM had lost their way completely and nearly went out of business. But for the appointment of Lou Gerstner."

"Lou quickly realised. It wasn't just about IBM's technology strategy. It was also to do with the culture of their people."

"You see. It was early in the internet age. IBM were still pushing mainframe technology and seemed too blinkered to see or care about the future."

"It was arrogance I suppose. Like they knew best. Which also came across in their people. The way they dealt with customers wasn't great at that time."

"Changing the technology and the way IBM delivered it to customers, although difficult, turned out to be the easy bit for Lou. By far the hardest job was changing the entire culture of such a huge corporation."

"Don't get me wrong Paul. None of it was easy and it took nearly a decade before Lou achieved success. When he left in

2002 IBM's share price had increased by 800% and it's stock market value had risen by $180 billion."

"WOW! The result and the numbers are amazing," gushed Paul.

"Yes, they are," agreed Athena. "Although the situation at IBM is not too dissimilar to yours Paul. Just on a larger scale."

"Due to technology and business model advances buying habits are changing. Just like what happened to IBM over 20 years ago. And if you don't change now (like IBM had too) you'll be dead in the water."

"To be honest Paul. There's more on the line for you than then for Lou Gerstner. If Lou failed it would be just his reputation that took a battering. If you fail, you'll lose everything, including your home." Athena winced.

"Which makes it even more critical we succeed," said Paul. His confidence was beginning to show.

"Let me update you with our progress," continued Paul. "After analysing the market, we've discovered families with school children, home workers and the self-employed are our target demographics."

"On average these demographics buy a set of printer cartridges four times a year and replace their printer every three years."

"What is also very interesting. Most bought expensive original cartridges to guarantee quality, usually from the supermarket whilst food shopping."

"Which means, on average, these demographics are spending around £280 annually on cartridges and printers."

"Great work!" exclaimed Athena. "Although, to make a huge statement and disrupt this marketplace, we've got to save them around 50%."

"That's exactly what I was thinking," confirmed Paul. "And do you know what, I think we can achieve it too."

"I've taken all the costs the team and I worked through and compiled them into a cost model," Continued Paul, removing his laptop from its case.

The laptop whirred into action, as Paul opened several spreadsheets and asked Athena to join him on his side of the table.

Excitedly Paul said; "as you can see" (using a pen to point) "We've got the figure to £11.99 a month and we even thought, to help cashflow, we'd offer the incentive of one month free for people willing to pay a year up front."

"The annual figure works out at £131.89, which is about a 53% saving against the current average annual spend of £280. Even people choosing to pay monthly will save £146 each year or 49%."

"This sounds great Paul. Please walk me through what you've included in the cost model?" asked Athena.

Paul clicked onto another spreadsheet, "the cost model is on a three-year replacement cycle. And includes a home rated wireless multi-function printer, twelve sets of replacement printer cartridges, delivery charges, extra costs for failures and enough margin to cover operational costs with a reasonable profit for our growth."

"Fantastic," smiled Athena. "Sounds like you've got most things covered. Have you thought about how people will order their replacement cartridges?"

"Yes," answered Paul. "Long term we want to send them out automatically. But that's going to take some clever and expensive software. Which at this stage we can't afford."

"For now, we'll give them two full sets of cartridges and once they've used one set, they can order a replacement set by phone, email or on any of our social channels and we'll deliver them for free."

"That sounds like a reasonable solution and a good service improvement target to head towards," replied Athena. "How will delivery happen?"

"This is where it gets interesting." Paul was excited to reveal the next stages of his plan. "To start with we think most customers will be pretty local to us, so we can deliver printers and replacement cartridges ourselves."

But if things take off, as we think they might and we get business from further afield, we'll then need to courier printers and post out cartridges."

"Yes. I agree with your approach" Athena cut in. "But one thing you must do before launch is test it all works. Order in a couple of the multifunction printers, together with the replacement cartridges you've chosen, and for the next two weeks test that it all works together."

"When we meet again in two weeks and everything's been tested, we'll discuss and agree the launch, together with a training plan for the team."

With that Paul packed away his laptop thanked Athena for her time and headed back to the Accrington store, where his office was located.

It just so happened that Don, Paul's most senior team member, managed the Accrington location. Making it the ideal place to carry out the testing.

"How'd it go with Athena," asked Don immediately on Paul's return.

"It went well," replied Paul. "The work the team put in last Saturday enabled the completion of the cost model, which we went through today."

"Athena thinks you've done a fantastic job and is really impressed with what we've developed. The only thing left is to test everything works seamlessly."

"Don, I'd like you to control the testing please?" asked Paul. "It's so critical to our success you're the only one I'd trust to do it right."

"Sure," confirmed Don. "What do you need me to do?"

"Please can you order 2 of the multifunction printers we've earmarked, and half dozen sets of the replacement cartridges we used in the cost model."

"When they arrive, hook one up to a system with a USB cable and set the other up wirelessly. Then test them continuously for print, scan and copy over the next 2 weeks, replacing the cartridges as required," said Paul.

Don carried out Paul's instructions to the most minute detail, continuously running the multi-function printers through their paces for the full two weeks.

The day of Paul's next strategy meeting with Athena came around quickly.

"What's the results Don?" Paul waited in anticipation.

"Great." Replied Don. "Everything's worked like a dream. No issue at all with print or copy quality, scanning has worked well and changing the empty cartridges for fresh ones has been hassle free. It gets a green light from me."

Paul was grinning like a Cheshire cat as he thanked Don, swung the door open and set off briskly to meet up with Athena.

Sat round the meeting room table with a coffee in one hand and a warm shortcake biscuit in the other, Paul was bursting inside.

"So, Paul." Started Athena. "How's the testing gone."

"Thought you'd never ask," said Paul smiling. "It's been brilliant."

"I gave the task to Don, as I knew, if he gave it a green light, the rest of the team will be on board too."

"Very astute Paul, well done!" Athena congratulated him. "Now it's time to discuss how we start selling the service."

"First, we need a very simple subscription sign up, something that's easy for the team to explain, is very secure and where the customer is in control."

"In a recent business venture, we came across a web based direct debit service called GoCardless, which also allows you to create subscriptions."

Athena brought up the service on her laptop; "It's simple to use Paul. First you need to register your company details and your business bank account, which will take a couple of days for GoCardless to check out and authorise."

"Once the account is open, you can setup monthly and annual subscription plans for the products you want. To start with, this will be two. A monthly and annual plan for your home printing service."

"Signing up customers is a doddle. Create a profile for each, add their name, address, email and attach a plan. GoCardless then pings them an email, asking them to register and to input their bank details for the subscription."

"Once the customer has completed the registration GoCardless pings you an email to confirm all is good. You can then deliver their printing service."

"It's very quick, slick and secure. They're authorised by the Financial Conduct Authority, all client communication is 256-bit SSL encrypted and they're ISO 27001 certified for information security."

"With GoCardless, you don't have to worry about the customers information, as GoCardless takes care of everything. Only customers can log into GoCardless to see or change their own bank details. Your team can't."

Athena continued. "Initially I see it working in three ways:

1) You'll sign customers up in store and they'll access their email on their phone or on an instore tablet to complete the set up.
2) You'll sign customers up in store and they'll go home to access their email in privacy to complete the set up.
3) You'll sign customers up over the phone or by email and they'll complete the set up at home.

Doesn't really matter how it happens, as long as customers are signing up."

"Once signed up, GoCardless automatically takes the pre-agreed amount monthly or annually, depositing it into your account within a few days. You'll then get an email showing who's paid and you simply send them a receipt."

"Blimey, that sounds easy," said Paul. "Now I just need to train the team."

"Changing mindsets won't be easy." Countered Athena. "You've got to be patient and persevere. But most of all, you've got to lead from the front."

"Get some leaflets designed that explain the service in very simple terms: which clearly state how much customers are likely to save, based on average annual usage. Listing all the other benefits they'll receive too."

"What do you mean Athena?" Paul posed the question with an air of bewilderment. "What other benefits?"

"I can't believe you've not thought about it," Athena laughed. "They're whole host of associated benefits they'll receive aside of the huge savings.

Things like:

1) A new multi-function printer
2) Unlimited replacement cartridges
3) Free delivery
4) Telephone support
5) A printer repair or replacement service
6) Printers refreshed every 3 years

In essence Paul, the customer is buying certainty and peace of mind. Certainty of their total printing costs and certainty if anything breaks, it will be fixed at no extra charge. Which leads to their total peace of mind."

"WOW. I've never thought about products in this way before Athena," stuttered Paul. "It's clearly going to be a big mindset change for me too."

"These benefits are what you need to train your team on Paul," started Athena. "They must be able to recite them with their eyes closed."

"Every customer coming into store must have the new printing service fully explained to them, including the savings and associated benefits. If they don't sign up in store, they must be given a leaflet to take home."

"Once you've embedded this process into your team, by directly showing them how it should be done with customers. I want you to leaflet all the housing estates within a three-mile radius of your store locations."

"Housing estates are where the majority of families with school children live, and where home workers and the self-employed are located."

"Have you been collecting customer data at all Paul?" asked Athena.

"Yes." Replied Paul. We've been running loyalty schemes for years. So, we've logged most customers' details, together with their transaction history. Why do you ask?"

"I've got another idea," said Athena. "Please can you arrange for each store manager to segment customers into an excel spreadsheet, those who buy two or more sets of replacement printer cartridges each year."

"And call them about the new printing service. Starting with those who buy four times a year, then three and then two. Even those buying cartridges twice a year will save a little and will still claim all the associated benefits."

"This is great Athena," smiled Paul. "I just know it's going to work."

"Paul. Let's not get ahead of ourselves," snapped back Athena. "Although very important. This is the first stage on the long road to recovery."

"Please remember. Our aim at this stage. Is to stabilise the business and stop customers defecting to buy cartridges from the supermarket or internet."

"It's very important you understand. In the short-term existing customer spend is going to drastically decrease, as you're saving them 50% on their previous spend. Making it vitally important you gain new customers too."

"You've got to implement these ideas immediately Paul, there's no time to lose. Creating a buzz and building momentum will take some time."

"Let's meet again in four weeks and you can update me on progress. In the meantime. I'll start to think about the next stage of your recovery."

With that, Paul packed his things away. He finished the last dregs of his coffee and slipped a biscuit into his pocket for the journey home, Hugged Athena thankfully and left to begin the critical make or break first phase of the recovery.

Chapter 5.   Operation business

It seemed like yesterday when Paul left Athena's to implement stage one of the recovery plan. And yet, he was sat in the very same seat one month on.

"Talk to me Paul." Commanded Athena. "How have things gone?"

Paul raised his head and looked into Athena's deep blue eyes. His own eyes started to well up and he couldn't stop the tears streaming down his cheeks.

The sheer emotion of the past month's activities suddenly erupted like a volcano. His salty tears stung like steaming hot lava.

Athena reached out and hugged Paul in that meaningful way, which immediately brought calm, as it had months earlier when they first met.

"It's okay Paul," consoled Athena. "I know it's tough, but you're not alone, I'm here with you to the end."

"Thank you, Athena," sniffed Paul. "This past month's been intense. I think it's the pressure of knowing our entire future relied on this bit working."

"Well did it?" Enquired Athena.

Paul looked again into her eyes. His own creased with an accomplished smile, saying; "Yes, it damn well did."

"What worked Paul? What are the numbers? Please share the story." Pleaded Athena excitedly.

"The first week was hard," began Paul. I spent it visiting stores in a continual cycle of training, showing, reinforcing, and encouraging."

"By the end of the week the team had grasped it and followed the training to the letter. Signing people up in store and over the phone. Whilst also working through the customer spreadsheets we'd compiled."

"They gave me the confidence to let them get on with it. Leaving me free and able to deliver the leaflets to the housing estates local to each store."

"By close of business yesterday we'd signed a hundred people onto the printing service. Half of which on annual contracts and forty being new customers."

"Which bodes well for the future. If half of sign ups pay up front for a year, it eases cash flow and helps fund those that pay monthly. 40% of sign-ups are new customers too, which is a very good sign and one we need to build on."

"Wonderful news Paul." Gasped Athena clapping her hands. "The challenge now is to maintain the momentum of the team, and you must also block out one full day each week in your diary for leafleting."

'Now it's time to begin phase two." Stated Athena.

"Phase two." Stuttered Paul. "We've only just started phase one. Shouldn't we be concentrating all our efforts on securing printing contracts with consumers."

Athena looked Paul square in the eyes saying. "Securing consumer business alone will not save you Paul. All we've done is to stop consumers leaving in droves to buy from the supermarket and online. It's bought us time to implement the entire strategy, which will stretch over many phases."

"Our strategy involves running multiple phases at once, spinning plates if you like. It's not ideal, but given the circumstances, it's got to happen."

"OK I get it Athena." Agreed Paul. "I'm just concerned doing too many things at once will have a negative effect on the team."

"Paul," Athena began. "I understand your concern. But given the circumstances. We have no choice."

"Your team though, will be much more resilient than you think. We must be open, honest, and transparent with them. In return they will do everything they can to help and probably come up with great ideas along the way too."

"So. What's next then?" Smiled Paul.

Athena started. "Phase two has to address your current reliance on consumers. Which means developing solutions for business and schools."

"Two things you must start doing immediately. The first is free delivery to all customers (including consumers and business) and the other is thirty-day business accounts."

"These two things, together with the savings you can provide against original manufactured cartridges, will attract businesses and primary schools."

"Don't get me wrong Paul," continued Athena. "Selling printer cartridges to businesses and schools is nowhere near the end game. But it's a start."

"Further down the line we'll have to introduce many more products and services, such as office supplies and business printing technology solutions."

"Yes," said Paul. "This makes complete sense Athena. Most business and primary schools will purchase original (OEM) printer cartridges, which will be put on accounts and delivered to them."

"If we can provide a similar service (swapping the OEM cartridges for our own brand aftermarket cartridges) whilst saving them 50% I think it'd work."

"I agree Paul. But you have to do more than saving 50%." Warned Athena.

"What do you mean?" Said a confused looking Paul.

"Business and schools will be more demanding," explained Athena. "Your product quality has to be consistently good and provide guarantees."

"The OEM cartridge manufacturers claim aftermarket cartridges are inferior, claiming poor print quality, not lasting as long and may even break printers."

"We have to address these claims head on," challenged Athena.

"What do you suggest?" quizzed Paul.

"It's simple Paul. You need to provide samples and guarantees. Samples to people who are unsure and a 100% money back satisfaction guarantee to combat quality or yield suggestions, with a guarantee you'll fix or replace malfunctioning printers caused by your cartridges," confirmed Athena.

"We know the quality and yield of our cartridges are at least as good as the OEM's." Stated Paul. "So, offering samples and guarantees makes sense."

"The question I suppose now is. How do we change things to incorporate a delivery service, manage the thirty-day accounts and make the business and school community aware of the new service delivery model?"

"Well Paul..." began Athena." It's time to make some very difficult decisions."

"What do you mean?" countered Paul.

Athena shot a look at Paul, which said I hope you're ready for this. "Burnley is by far your worst performing store and is costing you money. You only have one team member here, so it's the obvious one to close down."

"But I can't face making Chris redundant!" gasped Paul.

"I'm not saying that." Consoled Athena. "I'm saying, close Burnley to save money and make Chris the delivery person we need for the new service."

"Perfect," said a relieved Paul. "But. What about an accounts management system and how do we market the new service?"

"You've got an electronic point of sale (EPOS) system?" questioned Athena.

"Yes," replied Paul. "But we've only used it for consumer data and their associated transactions. We've never looked at what else it could provide."

"Well. That's where you start," said Athena. "If it doesn't provide what you need, speak to the developers, as there's likely an addon you can purchase."

"With regards to marketing. It's a similar approach to the leafleting you've been doing for the home service. Although it needs taking to another level."

"First. You need to design a handout pack. Which includes a leaflet about the service (including savings, delivery and payment on account) with contact details and the written guarantees you'll provide."

"Then it's time for bold calling, which is walking into business and schools, asking for your information to be passed to the correct person (making a note who this is) and then following it up with a phone call a few days later."

"You'll need to rely heavily on your team for the follow up and make sure a process is developed for this to happen. But it's going to take more effort from you visiting business and primary schools local to each store."

"I want you to have everything done and in place within the next 2 weeks. So, you can start bold calling. But make sure the follow up is in place too."

"Let's meet back at my place in three months. When I want a full report on the home printing package progress and the early results of the bold calling."

On leaving Athena's Paul went straight to the Burnley store to explain the next phase of their plans to Chris, seeking his acceptance of the new role.

"Oh, Hi Paul I wasn't expecting to see you today," said a surprised Chris.

"Hello Chris." Replied Paul. "Athena and I have been mapping out the next phase of changing our business model. Which requires your help."

Chris looked at Paul in a confused way not knowing what to say. So, Paul continued.

"We're going to start a free delivery service and providing thirty-day credit accounts to businesses and schools, to lessen our reliance on consumers."

"We require someone to operate the delivery service and to help grow the relationship with business and schools. We're hoping you would do it?"

"Wow," said Chris. "It sounds a great opportunity and I love meeting new people. But who'd look after the Burnley Store?"

"Well. Here's the thing," started Paul. "Burnley hasn't been doing so great and been losing money for months." So out of all the stores it's the obvious one to close, which frees you up to help grow the business side."

Chris smiled. "To be honest Paul. I was getting a bit fed up being on my own all day. This new opportunity sounds fun and perfect for me. I'm all in."

"Fantastic Chris!" beamed Paul. "It's going to take a couple of weeks to get things ready. I'll call a meeting tomorrow and bring the team up to speed."

The following day the team met after work at the Whitaker's Arms in Accrington. Paul had arranged some bar snacks and bought a round of drinks.

"Thanks for coming along," Paul began. "I want to thank you again for the hard work you're putting in to help change and reshape the business."

"Phase one (our home printing package) has started well. But it's very important we keep the momentum going. I'll be continuing with leafleting one day each week and want you to carry on selling and talking to all about it."

"It's time to introduce phase two; helping us lessen our reliance on consumers, by increasing our business and primary school customers."

"To do this, we're going to do two simple things," continued Paul. "Start a free delivery service for all customers and provide a thirty-day credit account facility for business and schools."

Paul looked around the table and saw the team slowly computing and digesting the information, before finally Don spoke up saying,

"I like the idea. Delivering our products will allow us to provide a faster service than the online sellers and gain customers back from supermarkets."

"Not only that," said Paul. "Most business and schools buy OEM cartridges. By providing credit accounts, 50% savings, product samples and guarantees we'll be able to win business off the traditional office supply companies."

"What do you mean by product samples and guarantees?" Asked Harry.

Paul explained to the team what Athena had advised.

"Business and schools will be more demanding. Our product quality must be consistently good, and we must provide guarantees, to build some trust."

"As you all know. The OEM cartridge manufacturers constantly claim aftermarket cartridges are inferior, give poor print quality, print less pages and may even cause printers to break."

"To address these claims head on we must provide samples and guarantees."

"Samples to people who are unsure and a 100% money back satisfaction guarantee to combat quality or yield suggestions. Together with a guarantee we'll fix or replace malfunctioning printers caused by our cartridges."

"Listen. We know quality and yield of our cartridges are as good as OEM's," confirmed Paul. "So, offering samples and guarantees makes sense."

"Yes. I get it," agreed Harry. "We do this already when we need to convince people in the shop who want an OEM. On occasions we'll give them a free sample to try and then the next time they'll buy our own brand."

"I suppose we guarantee our cartridges without it being officially written down," added Barry. "We always give a full refund if someone is unhappy."

"But we've never agreed to fix or replace printers before," explained Adele.

"Have we ever had to due to our cartridges causing the problem?" probed Paul.

The team quizzed each other before Don confirmed. "Not directly caused by our cartridges."

"Why not offer it as a guarantee then?" Replied Paul. At which point the entire team nodded and confirmed their agreement.

Steph, who works at the Blackburn store, then mumbled whilst stuffing a samosa into her mouth; "so, how's it going to work then?"

"I'm glad someone's eating the food," laughed Paul. Which broke the tension. Leading the rest of team to relax and tuck into the food too.

"OK. I've got an announcement to make." All eyes turned on Paul. "Chris has agreed to be in charge of deliveries and to help build customer relationships."

Jaws dropped, silence rang out for a few seconds, before Don began; "but what about the Burnley store."

"As I said to Chris yesterday," explained Paul. "Burnley hasn't been doing so great and been losing money for months, so it's the obvious one to close."

"We certainly didn't want to let Chris go and introducing the new delivery and credit account model, presents him with a new opportunity."

Chris jumped in. "Guys don't worry about me, I'm well happy. I was getting a bit down working on my own. I'm a people person and this suits me better."

The team seemed at ease, so Paul carried on. "There's a few other things, which we've got to develop quickly, and I'll need your help please."

"Tim, you're good with designing stuff. Would you be able to design a handout pack? Including a leaflet that shows savings, delivery, and account terms. Together with the 100% satisfaction and fix or replace guarantees."

"Sure-thing boss," replied Tim.

"Steph, you're our IT guru and we need you to look into our EPOS system. We need to understand if it'll allow us to manage credit account customers, produce invoices, statements and has a basic debt management facility."

"I'm all over it," replied Steph.

"Steph, Tim, I need this completed in two weeks please," added Paul. "During this time, I'll work up a spreadsheet for each store to keep track of your opportunities and to keep score of the numbers, so we can review weekly."

"In two weeks, I'll be spending three days a week bold calling. Which is walking into business and schools, passing our information to the correct person (making a note who this is) and then following up with a phone call a few days later."

"Don, Harry and Barry: As the store managers, I'll be expecting you to make sure the bold calls for your area are followed up with a phone call, quotes are produced and followed up and meetings are carried out when requested."

"Every Friday I'll visit each store. Where we'll review your business and school customer development scorecard and measure your home printing package conversions. Are you clear with this?" Finished Paul.

Don, Harry, and Barry looked at each other, nodded and turned back to Paul saying in unison; "crystal."

Two weeks passed in a blur and the team met back at the Whitaker Arms. As the last time. Again, Paul laid on plenty of bar snacks and got in a round of drinks.

Something was different this time. The buzz of voices from the team populated the air, they chatted excitedly and immediately dived into the large spread of bar snacks.

"Thank you all for making the time to attend," Paul began. "This evening's about understanding our progression and agreeing on the next steps."

"Tim, please can I have your design work update?" Asked Paul.

"Absolutely Paul." responded Tim. "Artwork is completed. The rest of the team has already reviewed it, we've tweaked it where necessary. I've brought them along for your final review before printing."

Tim passed the documents over. Paul told the team to carry on without him, whilst he spent 10 minutes or so reviewing the artwork. He saw the future of a successful model cast upon the page in shades of blue.

"Fantastic work Tim. Well done." Paul congratulated him. "And thank you to everyone for helping Tim and contributing to the final versions. They're perfect."

"Your turn Steph - how've you got on with updating the EPOS system?"

"It wasn't as bad as I thought Paul," smiled Steph. "I found the existing system had the functionality already built in. I just needed a bit of training from the developers, which I've now shared with the team."

"Wow!" gasped Paul. "Great news. Thanks, Steph. Scorecards are completed too. We've progressed quickly and we're ready to start."

"My weekly diary is. Monday's delivering home printing leaflets. Tuesday, Wednesday, and Thursday is bold calling one day for each store. Friday is our review day, with some time for me to catch up on paperwork."

For the next three months Paul worked closely with his team. Supporting each store with leafleting and bold calling, using each Friday to review progress, embrace the learnings and train the team to become better and stronger.

Chris embraced his new role. Not just delivering. Providing an advice service for customers. It really helps having some technical knowledge too, enabling him to solve minor problems as he delivers goods. Great customer service.

It was nearing time for Paul's three-month review with Athena, and he was going through the store's scorecards, gathering the key information Athena will want. The numbers looked good. Paul expected a positive meeting.

Chapter 6.   Nearly fatal attraction

Something seemed different. Paul moved towards the entrance. The door was ajar. He shouted. "Hey, Athena, It's Paul."

But there was no reply. Paul edged through the open door into the huge hallway. The grand staircase, which led to the rooms on the first floor, loomed large in front of him.

Paul called out again. "Athena. It's Paul, I'm here for our review meeting."

Noises echoed down the staircase. Someone was upstairs. Paul thought he better check it out, Athena might be in trouble.

On reaching the first floor, Paul identified the noise was coming from a room at the end of the hallway on the left. He made his way slowly and quietly down the hallway until he came to a stop outside the room.

He knocked on the door and called out. "Athena. It's Paul is everything OK." Again, his calls were met with silence, except for this continuing noise.

Paul reached for the doorknob, turned it, and pushed the door open. The room was empty, but the noise continued. It sounded like heavy rainfall and seemed to be coming from a door at the far end of the room.

Paul quietly made his way across the room to the door and knocked, whilst calling out Athena's name once again. But still no reply.

Reaching for knob Paul turned it and slowly opened the door. The noise became clear; it was the sound of a very powerful shower. The room was so full of steam Paul had to feel his way around.

Paul was beginning to panic. A horrible feeling sent a shudder through his body. What if something terrible had happened to Athena. He was terrified of what he may find deep in the steam-strewn room.

Eventually he reached what seemed to be a large glass door, which Paul thought would lead to the shower. Paul flung the door open, to be met by a figure who let out a huge shriek and punched Paul square in the nose, sending him backwards and knocking him unconscious.

Squinting and rubbing his eyes, everything looked blurred and his nose was throbbing like when he'd hit his thumb with a lump hammer. Paul was laid down on a plush bed with an ice pack on his forehead.

His vision was returning, and he could just make out the figure of Athena in a long white silk bathrobe. "Paul," Athena said. "You must forgive me."

"Wwww what do you mean?" Paul stammered.

"I didn't realise it was you. I couldn't see clearly through the steam. I thought I was going to be attacked, so I just lashed out," cried Athena.

Paul now coming to his senses said, "Don't cry Athena. It's completely my fault. The front door was open and when you didn't respond to my calls, I was worried something bad had happened. So, I came looking for you."

"Jesus though. I don't think you need any help from me, as you pack one hell of a punch. I'm no lightweight, but you took me completely off my feet."

Paul's mind began to wander. Athena seemed to be looking younger, her hair wasn't as grey, and her body looked firm and muscular.

His mind thought back to the moment in the bathroom. Through the steam he faintly made out the body shape of Athena. She was magnificent. So toned and muscular. Not what he'd imagined for an older lady.

"Paul, Paul are you ok." Athena called worryingly.

Paul quickly snapped out of his dream like state. "I'm ok, don't worry. Think I'm in a bit of shock or I've got a little concussion." Paul chuckled.

"Don't Paul." Athena pleaded. "I feel bad enough already."

"Honestly, I'm ok," reassured Paul. "Get yourself dressed. I'll put the coffee on. It's time for us to crack on with the task at hand."

Twenty minutes later Paul and Athena sat in their usual spot, with fresh coffee in hand. But not a shortbread biscuit in sight.

"Why did you leave the front door open anyway Athena," questioned Paul.

"Well. I was running late, and I'd only just got back after spending the last twenty-four hours travelling and sleeping on planes." Explained Athena. "I was in desperate need of a shower, so I decided to leave the door open for you."

"Anyway, that's enough small talk." Athena focused. "All's well that ends well and no bones were broken. Now it's time to report on progress."

"The team got on board straight away." Started Paul. "I was most nervous about closing Burnley and asking Chris to be in charge of deliveries and help to build our customer relationships."

"I've learnt though. Things are never as bad as they first seem. Chris was pleased. He was lonely and demotivated being stuck out on his own."

"In fact. He was my biggest advocate when discussing the new business service with the rest of the team. He made the discussions much easier."

"How was setting up the new systems and designing the handout packs?" questioned Athena.

"Had it all completed within two weeks," smiled Paul. "The team really stepped up and took on the responsibility, whilst I built opportunity spreadsheets, so each store can manage prospects and keep score."

Whilst explaining Paul took out his laptop and opened a spreadsheet titled 'Master Scorecard' and positioned it where they both could see.

"Each store has its own scorecard on these separate tabs, which feed into this master scorecard." Began Paul. "We're measuring the number of bold calls, successful follow up calls, meetings secured, quotations generated, quotation follow ups and new customers won."

"Sounds good. But what are the numbers Paul?" Asked Athena.

"Be patient Athena," winked Paul. "I'm getting to them."

"We're averaging about thirty bold calls a week for each store. So, ninety in total. Meaning over a thousand bold calls in the last three months. With seven hundred successful follow up calls, fifty meetings and two hundred quotations. Leading to ninety new customers."

"That's great." Exclaimed Athena. "But what about financials."

"Average customer order value has been fifty pounds, and it looks like customers are likely to purchase bi-monthly, as the majority of month one customers purchased again in month three," said Paul.

"To date project revenue is six thousand pounds with 50% gross margin," continued Paul. "Working on the same quarterly figures and three hundred and sixty new customers. Our twelve-month projection is sixty thousand in revenue with a 50% gross margin."

"Thank you, Paul," smiled Athena. "Please can you update me on the home printing solution."

Paul flicked to another spreadsheet. "If you remember. In the first month we had a hundred new sign ups. 40% were new customers and 50% paid a year up front."

"Since then we've had another two hundred sign ups. But it's flipped. 60% were new customers, although 50% are still paying a year up front."

"The flips not surprising Paul." Started Athena. "And neither is the reduction in sign up rates."

"It was always going to be easier to sign up existing customers as opposed new ones. It seems you've now signed up most existing customers. So, don't be surprised when the new sign up numbers reduce further."

"Paul," Athena continued. "You and your team are doing a fantastic job. Probably better than I expected. But be warned. Don't let complacency set it. You're nowhere near out of the woods yet."

"I know you've got weekly reviews set up. Make sure these continue and drill right down into the conversion rates. If you can improve these by even a couple of percent, it can make a huge difference to the numbers."

"It's time for phase three Paul." Athena Grinned, Paul could see the excited anticipation for the coming months in her face. "Are you ready?"

"Bring it on!!" challenged Paul.

"We need a way of increasing the average transaction value of business customers," the goddess began. "If we can double it from fifty to a hundred pounds, both your revenue and gross profit will double from this group of customers."

"Agreed," said Paul. "But how the hell can we do that?"

"Well," Athena mused aloud. "Currently you're very limited in what you have available to sell to business customers, mainly just printer cartridges"

"Let's not forget the goal of providing office technology products to small and medium enterprises in an affordable subscription model."

"To achieve this, It's not all about technology. You've got to supply the basics too: Things like stationery, general office products, workplace solutions and even office furniture. So, let's start there."

"A while back, I did some strategy work with the Office Depot executive board in the states. By introducing some new specially chosen product lines, we tripled the average spend of their top ten thousand customers."

"Yes. I know, they're a massive company! And they don't really have a focus on technical office services, but the principles still remain the same."

"It's not just as simple as going to ten or twenty different suppliers to get everything we'll need. Being so small, you won't get competitive pricing or great service from them."

"We'll need to partner with a buying group. Not just any buying group Paul. You need to do due diligence and choose a buying group who has the right suppliers, can offer competitive prices, but most of all have a similar ethos."

"Got it," said Paul, charged with a new sense of determination. "Although I'm not sure where to start."

"Google them." Replied Athena. "But that won't give you everything you need. Once you've got a list, ring some of their members. Tell them you may join. Ask them about supplier prices, fees and how they get treated."

"We've got to get this bit nailed quickly before we can start implementing phase three. Let's meet again in two weeks, we'll map out the next steps then."

With that Paul packed his stuff away. He thanked Athena and made his way back through the towering marble columns, to the next rung of his climb.

It was very late. On the journey home Paul's mind wandered back to the bathroom incident. He still couldn't believe how toned and muscular Athena had looked and the strength she had to knock him out cold.

When they had first met many months earlier. Although she was a very elegant lady, he was sure Athena was in her seventies. Now though, she seemed ten years younger and Paul felt a strange attraction towards her.

Two weeks passed in a blink of an eye. Paul stood outside Athena's magnificent home. This time the front door was closed. Somewhere deep inside Paul felt a tinge of disappointment. Thinking back to what happened previously.

He rang the bell. The door flung open. Athena stood in the doorway. Dressed in a long white silk gown. Her deep blue eyes blazing with arms open and a welcoming smile.

"Come in Paul." Athena enthused. "I've got fresh coffee brewing and warm shortbread waiting. I showered earlier," she said with a twinkle in her eye.

"So. Tell me. How have you got on?"

Paul took a sip of the hot fresh coffee, placed the cup back on its saucer and said. "You were right. It wasn't as straightforward as I thought."

"Most buying groups were in it for themselves. Each provided similar pricing agreements with the same suppliers and similar support packages, but the relationship they had with their members differed greatly."

"After talking to many members and a select number of buying groups, only one stood out. Much is similar between them all, except for their ethos; the relationship between buying group and member."

"The Nemo Group seems to be one big family. With full members being part owners in a kind of co-operative. Excess profits are shared with full members and on most occasions, pay their annual membership fees."

"Although we'll initially join as affiliate members (paying a reduced annual fee and not sharing in the profits,) as we grow, we can upgrade to full membership and take advantage of the extra benefits this brings."

"Sounds like you've chosen wisely," smiled Athena. "Now down to business."

"Before we map out phase three, I want to educate you about the underhand tactics that some larger national office supply company's practice."

"When trying to win business, they ask for the customer's basket of most popular products. They price these very competitively (sometimes less than their cost price). But other products outside of this are charged at twice or even three times the normal sell price, which makes them loads of profit overall."

"This is not you Paul. You provide simple honest service. You're uncomplicated and simple to do business with. Transparent and honest in everything you do. Being fair and reasonable with all prices. Providing a service where customers go, 'WOW!' Making them tell others all about you."

"Never get drawn into this dark world, where other suppliers hoodwink customers into thinking they're getting a great deal. It's a slippery slope."

"The team and I could never do this Athena," said a stunned Paul. "It's not part of our identity. Our team's been built on honesty, taking responsibility, and always doing the right thing. This will never change."

"We'll set fair and reasonable prices, with set margins across the board on all products made available through the buying group. Our customers can be sure they will not be hoodwinked on any products they purchase from us."

"That's exactly what I want to hear Paul," confirmed Athena. "It's time to map out phase three."

"What selling tools do the Nemo Group provide?" Asked Athena.

"They can provide a physical catalogue, a virtual catalogue and even an ecommerce website. As well as paying a small monthly membership fee, you must pay for these other resources too," explained Paul.

"In addition, they have quite a number of free resources available on their intranet site. Things like letters, quotation forms and leaflet templates."

"I've detailed all the resources and relevant costs in this spreadsheet," said Paul as he pulled out his laptop.

Athena glanced over the spreadsheet. "The costs are reasonable for the resources and we'll get a good ongoing return on the monthly investment."

"Paul. I want you to order a thousand of the catalogues and arrange for Nemo to get you up and running with an eCommerce website," started Athena

"I'm right in thinking that the eCommerce site mirrors what's in the physical catalogue and allows you to set your own margins."

"Correct," confirmed Paul.

"Great," enthused Athena. "Chris won't be able to do this on his own, as well as managing deliveries. The store managers are needed for this one."

"Your focus on bold calling and leafleting has to continue, as does the follow up calls, quotations and meetings that the team carry out."

"The difference being: Once you've won a new business or school customer and Chris has delivered their first order. The relevant store manager must call them and arrange to provide a free assessment to identify other areas of their operation where we can help them save money."

"You'll need to design an assessment form to provide the store managers with a script to run through, allowing them to collate all the customer's product information, with their current prices."

"Before they leave, the store managers must then book another appointment a few days later, to present the customer's savings proposal."

"At this point. Customers can be set up with an eCommerce account. Giving them access to the full product range with prices, online or in the catalogue. From there, they can either order online, email to you or ring the order through."

"Do this correctly and this will easily double your customer's average transaction values. We'll meet again in three months." Athena confidently finished.

7.   An unexpected thief

Startled, Paul woke to the sound of his mobile buzzing on the bedside table. It was 8am on Sunday; The only day he would normally have a lie in.

Don's name was flashing up on the screen. A little worried. Paul quietly and quickly exited the bedroom before answering.

"Paul. I'm really sorry for ringing you so early on a Sunday." Don's seemingly panicked voice vibrated through the handset. "I've not slept all night."

"What's up?" Paul asked with real concern.

"Yesterday morning. Ewan asked to borrow my car to get to the post office before it closed, as he had a couple of parcels he needed to urgently post."

"Go on," prompted Paul.

"The thing is," stuttered Don. "Driving home I found two packets of Epson cartridges left in the footwell. They could only have been left by Ewan."

"Borrowing my car, going to the post office and Epson cartridges left in my car, raised my suspicions on so many levels," he explained.

"When I got home. I was straight on eBay, searching for the Epson cartridges. Eventually (after a while) I came across

Ewan's seller profile. Which was listing these Epson cartridges and other similar things too."

Paul was shocked. "You think Ewan's been stealing stock to sell on eBay Don?" Paul blurted out.

"Exactly," confirmed Don. "If I were unsure, I wouldn't say anything. But the evidence is crystal clear Paul."

"My loyalty lies with you and the business Paul. Although I like and work with Ewan. I could never allow anything like this to happen. It's just wrong."

"You know Ewan does most of the purchasing for all three stores, and it just seems the temptation has gotten too great for him to handle."

Paul grabbed a pad and detailed down the information Don had found on eBay. Including types, number of products sold, and the amounts involved.

"What are you going to do Paul?" asked Don.

"I'm going to spend today looking at our supplier purchases to tie them up with Ewan's eBay sales, and total up exactly how much he's stolen."

"First thing on Monday, I'll be at the police station to present the evidence to them, and we'll see what they suggest we do next."

Paul thanked Don for his loyalty and for gathering the information, taking time to reassure him. Making sure he'd say nothing to Ewan on Monday.

Paul spent most of Sunday going over paperwork, matching Ewan's eBay sales with the orders Ewan had made with their suppliers.

Ewan's stealing had been happening for about a month, which explains why Paul hadn't spotted it yet. Eventually he'd have spotted it, when it came time to pay the suppliers at the end of the following month.

In total Ewan stole fifteen hundred pounds worth of goods and in some cases, sold it on eBay for less than the price it cost the business to buy them. Paul was fuming and more than ready to meet with the police the following morning.

The interview room was small, dimly lit and smelt a bit stale. There was a row of small windows high up at the far end of the room. In the centre was a large brown well used table with four unmatching chairs.

Two of the chairs were occupied. Police officer Rose sat in one. Whilst Paul sat directly across from him.

"Right Paul, please start from the beginning- providing as much detail and evidence as you can," commanded officer Rose.

Paul began explaining everything. Starting with Don finding cartridges in his car. Ewan's eBay selling profile and the supplier orders Ewan had made.

The information was backed up with printouts of Ewan's selling profile, copies of the supplier purchases Ewan had made, including Paul's spreadsheet, which matched the eBay product sales to the supplier invoices.

Office Rose took some time to consider things and said, "The evidence is clear Paul, there is no doubt Ewan has committed a serious offence. It's time to arrest him and bring him into the station for questioning."

Paul was shocked. He knew Ewan had done wrong and if he'd continued, it would have had dire consequences on the business. At the same time however, he felt a tinge of sorrow and even pity for Ewan.

Paul came to his senses, believing Ewan needed to learn from this and take responsibility for his own actions. He had potentially put the livelihoods of his fellow work colleagues at risk, let alone stealing from his employer.

Officer Rose was waiting patiently. Eventually Paul asked, "please could you give me about an hour before you arrive, as I need to detail a suspension letter and make sure Ewan gets it before you take him away."

"Absolutely," agreed officer Rose.

Paul burst out of the police station in a mild panic. Jumped in his car and sped to the Accrington store.

Walking in the store Paul said. "Good morning." To Don, Ewan, and Tim. "I've just got to nip upstairs to do something urgently. Please don't disturb me."

Paul bolted up the stairs, sweat forming on his brow and quickly closed the office door behind him.

The anxiety was overwhelming. Paul took some deep breaths and began to calm down. He sat at his desk and searched for the information he needed for Ewan's suspension letter.

Ewan was to be suspended on full pay, pending an investigation into stealing products to sell on eBay, and would be invited to a disciplinary hearing to discuss the issue.

Paul had just finished printing the letter when the familiar sound of the shop door being opened rang out, echoing upstairs.

Don went to the counter to be met by two police officers, one of which was officer Rose.

Officer Rose in a deep Lancashire accent asked. "Please can I speak with Ewan."

"I'll just fetch him," replied Don.

Ewan sheepishly appeared from the back room to face the police officers.

Officer Rose immediately began. "Ewan. I'm arresting you for stealing products worth fifteen hundred pounds and selling them on eBay for personal gain."

"You do not have to say anything. But it may harm your defence if you do not mention when questioned something which you later rely on in court. Anything you do say, may be given in evidence."

With that, officer Rose put the handcuffs on and the two officers marched Ewan out to the police van. As they helped Ewan inside, Paul appeared and asked if he could speak to Ewan. The two officers agreed.

Paul took a deep breath. "I'm sorry it has come to this Ewan. This letter suspends you from work on full pay, pending an investigation and invites you to a disciplinary hearing on Thursday evening to discuss the issue. Whilst being suspended I must take back your keys to the store please."

With that, speechless, Ewan handed Paul his keys. The officers slammed the van doors shut and sped off towards the police station.

That evening officer Rose called Paul, "we've interviewed Ewan this afternoon and it's clear he's guilty. Although currently he's not admitting anything."

"As he still lives at home, we decided to take him there to explain the situation to his parents, telling him and them that Ewan must come back to the station on Wednesday for a further interview."

"After spending some time with his parents, I've got no doubt they'll make him see sense and he'll admit everything to us on Wednesday."

Paul thanked officer Rose for the update, and they agreed to speak again on Wednesday.

Wednesday arrived along with Paul's anxiety. He couldn't concentrate on his bold calling activity and was keen to understand the outcome of the interview before the disciplinary hearing on Thursday evening.

Eventually his phone rang. It was officer Rose. "Paul. Some good news and some bad news. Ewan's come clean and admitted everything."

"That's great officer Rose. What's the bad news." Questioned Paul.

"Well. We took it to the CPS (Crown Prosecution Service) to get their approval for a court date. But because it's his first offence they have advised to give him an 'on record' caution."

"He's been up in front of the commanding officer today, where his caution has been read out and documented on his record."

Paul was deflated. He was keen to get the money back for the stolen goods, through the judicial court system. But there was no chance of this now.

Officer Rose continued; "listen Paul. I'm disappointed too. I know you were hoping to get compensated, all I can suggest, is to try the civil courts."

"Yes. I am disappointed. But thank you for the advice." Admitted Paul. "I've got a disciplinary hearing with Ewan booked in for tomorrow night too."

"If I'm honest Paul. Now Ewan's pleaded guilty. It's very unlikely he'll turn up. Please don't let it worry you," reassured Officer Rose.

Although Paul was ready and waiting in his office, Thursday night was a no show. Paul took the time available to detail a letter to Ewan confirming the decision and bring his employment to an end, which he delivered by hand.

It was time to put this behind him, move on and begin implementing the phase three plans.

Chapter 8.   Bursting

Paul invited his three store managers (Don, Harry, and Barry) to a brainstorming meeting straight after work at a local Chinese restaurant.

The Sun Dragon was housed in an odd building for a restaurant. Paul remembered it well from his youth. It was a snooker and pool club.

Paul had met with his managers here in the past. It wasn't the most inviting restaurant he'd ever been too. But the family who ran it were very friendly, the food was okay, it was a fair price and it was usually quiet.

Arriving first, Paul ordered for them all, he knew the others would want a round of mixed starters to share and a bottle of Tsingtao Chinese beer.

Once everyone had arrived and started tucking in Paul began. "Thank you all for coming, I genuinely appreciate it, as it's eating into your personal time."

Barry quipped. "No worries Paul. I'd go anywhere for free Chinese," whilst the other two laughed along.

Paul smiled before carrying on. "It's time for us to implement phase three of our plans, and I need your help doing it."

"What do we need to do Paul?" Questioned Harry.

Paul explained about joining Nemo (the buying group) and all the different office and workplace products, they'll be able to get at market leading prices.

Even firing up his laptop to show them the eCommerce website, whilst explaining how the products in the catalogue link back to the website.

Finally. Paul got round to the logistics of making it work. "Guys. I need you to carry out the product and price assessments with customers."

"Chris is going to be way too busy delivering the products. He just won't have the time to spend assessing customer products and prices too."

The store managers looked at each other. Don knew what they were all thinking and decided to speak up. "We'll do it Paul. But we're going to need some support too."

"What did you have in mind Don?" quizzed Paul.

"At the moment," Don began. "We're ringing, quoting and following up all the organisations you're bold calling, as well as ringing consumers about the home printing service."

"We've also lost a team member in Ewan. So, our time is extremely stretched. The rest of the team are busy looking after our store customers, so they can't help us either."

Paul agreed. "Yes. I can see the issue. Look guys. I'm sorry I didn't foresee this problem. Have you got any suggestions as to what we can do?"

Don answered. "I think we can get by without directly replacing Ewan. But we'll need to use his salary to employ someone who can run the sales process for the bold calling and home printing service."

"This will free us up to spend more time developing existing business customers, doing the assessments and making sure our service is spot on."

"What do you think, Barry and Harry?" Both nodded in agreement.

"I agree too," confirmed Paul. "But who do we know and trust to do it?"

"Well," said Don. "You know, Belinda: my sister. She already does something similar for a software company in Rawtenstall and she was only saying last week she fancied a change, because it was hard managing the kids too."

"This is something she could easily do from home, which would really help her out too. I'll discuss it with her over the weekend and let you know."

With that. They finished the remaining starters, polished off their Chinese beer and departed into the night for a well-earned weekend break.

It was Sunday. Paul's mobile was ringing. Don's voice sounded, calmer than it was when Paul was awoken last week. Paul had been up ages and was enjoying a coffee.

"Morning Don." Paul Answered. "What can I help you with."

"I spoke with Belinda last night about the opportunity," Don said excitedly. "She's really interested and would like to meet you to discuss it further."

"That's fantastic news," smiled Paul. "Please can you text me her number."

As soon as Belinda's number came through, Paul was on the phone and arranged to meet up at her house that same afternoon.

"Hi Paul. Please come in," started Belinda. "You've met Teddy haven't you."

Teddy was Belinda's husband and worked for Konica Minolta. Paul knew him from school years ago, although Teddy was a good bit younger.

"Hi Teddy," Paul, shook his hand. "I've not seen you since school."

"Yes, I remember." Replied Teddy. "It's a long time ago, if I remember you were 3 years above me."

"Would you like a coffee Paul?" asked Belinda.

"Yes please. Black no sugar," answered Paul.

The scent of coffee filled the air, as Paul and Belinda went and sat in her conservatory. It was quiet and private from the rest of the house. With a large wooden table with chairs at one end and a sofa and wall mounted television at the other.

"Obviously, Don told you that I'm interested in the position." Began Belinda.

"I do like my job, but it's getting harder to work in the office when I've got young children to manage as well. So, working from home really appeals to me."

"It's not just about the money Paul. But I'd need at least what I'm paid now with a similar commission structure. And if we can agree on this, the working from home makes it a no brainer for me."

"But I've not even explained what I'd like you to do yet Belinda," said a surprised Paul.

"Don's already filled me in. He's explained I'll be required to run the new business sales process and sell the home printing package to consumers."

"Listen Paul. I've done this job for years, if I do so say so myself, I'm pretty good at it. Everything will be documented, and we'll have a review meeting once a week. Don't worry. If I need help. I'll ask one of the team."

Paul didn't know what to say. He was impressed. They spent the next hour discussing things in more detail and agreed on a financial package.

Belinda's notice period was 2 weeks, which was perfect timing. Paul needed this time to design the assessment forms, sign the Nemo agreement, help set up the eCommerce website and order the catalogues.

Two weeks later Paul arrived back at Belinda's house. With him he had a laptop, phone, and other stationery products that Belinda needed.

They spent the morning training, going over systems and fine tuning the sales process and communication channels. Then it was time to start.

Tuesday the store managers began making assessment appointments with existing business customers.

Paul reverted to his routine. Three days bold calling (one for each store) and one day leafleting homes. Friday was free for reviews and paperwork.

Belinda hit the ground running. It was like she'd worked in the business for years. She already knew most of the team through Don. It was like a family.

It was time for the reviews. It had only been a week. But there were early signs the strategy to increase business transaction values was working.

The store managers had already carried out twelve assessments collectively. Which had resulted in eight quotations for products from the new range. Two sales had already happened with the other six still pending.

And Belinda was on fire. The store managers had many other tasks to do. Meaning calls, quotations and sales were squeezed into two hours each day.

Belinda though, spent the entire day doing just this. So could do the work of all three of them put together, and a fair bit more. She was very efficient.

In four days, Belinda had made two hundred calls, sent twenty quotations, won five new business customers, signed up six home printing packages and arranged three very promising appointments for the store managers.

Since Ewan had departed. Each store had taken responsibility for their own purchasing. It wasn't ideal, as it was attracting extra delivery charges.

With stretched resources and a need to have products available the next morning, so they could be delivered later that same day. It had to happen this way.

Over the next four weeks the same trends continued: more assessments, more telephone calls, more quotations, more orders, and more new customers.

All sorts of products were turning up at the stores to be delivered out to customers. As well as stationery. There was tea, coffee, cleaning products, toilet roll and packaging materials.

Paul thought it was going great. Until desks, chairs, cupboards and filing cabinets started showing up. The stores were bursting with products.

It was only month two of phase three and Paul had to hire a bigger van at least once a week, sometimes twice! By the end of month two, he'd had enough and bought a bigger van on finance.

The quarter was coming to an end and Paul was worried they would soon implode. The small retail stores were just not fit for purpose anymore.

The team had done everything he'd asked of them and much more. Belinda had been a revelation, making Paul wish he'd employed her years ago.

The final quarter review was complete, and Paul collated the numbers ready to meet with Athena. But he knew something else had to drastically change.

Chapter 9.   The Big Move

It was Saturday, the sun was shining, the birds singing. Paul was both excited and apprehensive when he pulled into Athena's courtyard.

Reaching the front porch Paul noticed a hand-written note on the door. It said, 'Paul, I'm in the back garden.' With a large arrow pointing to the right.

Paul made his way round to the back of this huge mansion. Eventually finding himself staring out at an oasis; There were trees, rivers, lakes, waterfalls, fountains, and statues within what seemed, miles of open field.

In the distance he could see a large white tent and a figure brandishing, what seemed to be a large sword glinting against the sunlight.

The figure was moving at pace thrashing this way and that with the sword. And seemed to be wearing a thick black mask and figure-hugging body suit.

As Paul eased tentatively closer, he recoginsed the figure. It was Athena. Although her hair was no longer grey. It was now more jet black.

He watched her move. She was amazing: Twisting and turning. Jumping and crouching. Thrusting the sword at empty spaces like her life depended on it.

Paul made sure he didn't get too close; he didn't fancy getting his head decapitated. He kept a safe distance and just admired the scene.

Athena had changed so much since they first met. Gone was the white grey hair, aging face, and frail appearance. She now appeared much younger, stronger, with an agile and amazing body shape.

Paul thought back to the bathroom incident, where he first noticed how Athena was changing. Feeling the same attraction stir within him again.

Athena woke Paul out of his dream state shouting. "Paul, come on over." Finishing her exercise, she'd removed the mask and saw he had arrived.

Paul went to meet Athena in the open space. On the floor were lots of large padded exercise mats, arranged in a large square. To the side was the white tent. Inside was a table laid with water, fruit, and a whole host of weapons.

"Good to see you Paul." Began Athena giving him a close hug.

Paul could feel her muscular and athletic body holding him tight, whilst feeling her warmth radiating through him.

Composing himself Paul smiled back saying. "It's great to see you too and I've really missed our discussions. But. Can I ask what you've been doing?"

"What this?" Athena laughed, pointing to the face mask and weapons.

"Yes." Replied Paul with another smile. "I was watching you. You're amazing. I mean, what you were doing was amazing. The way you moved."

"This is my exercise routine," explained Athena. "Ancient warfare really interests me, and I'm highly trained in using these types of weapons."

"Instead of doing gym work like most people to keep in shape, I use virtual reality (VR) technology and fight all kinds of mythical monsters. It allows me to improve my weaponry skills, whilst keeping in shape."

"Would you like a quick go Paul?" grinned Athena.

"Sure thing," replied Paul excitedly.

Athena set up the VR on its easiest setting. Programming in a battle with a Roman gladiator in an exact replica of the Colosseum in Rome.

Paul put the mask on. Athena started the program. It was amazing. He stood in Rome's Colosseum, filled to the rafters with a baying crowd.

Facing him was his opponent. He seemed seven-foot-tall, complete with body armour and helmet, wielding the biggest sword Paul had ever seen.

It's only a game, Paul kept saying to himself. But it all seemed so real. The gladiator made his move and slashed at Paul with the massive sword.

Paul quickly moved to the right, making his opponent miss and stumble. Giving Paul an opportunity to swing his own (much smaller) sword, catching the gladiator clean across the throat.

The gladiator dropped to the floor with blood gushing out of the wound, within seconds it was over. The crowd roared and Paul won his freedom.

Removing his mask and turning to Athena. "Wow. I've never experienced anything like that. It all seemed so real."

"It's great isn't it. I use it every day. Even taking it away on trips with me, minus the weapons of course," winked Athena. "Come on Paul. Let's go inside. Please can you sort the coffee, whilst I have a quick shower."

"Sure." Replied Paul, whilst thinking. "Oh no! Not the shower again."

Ten minutes later they were sat in their usual spot at the meeting table, coffee in hand.

"Right." Started Athena. "You go first Paul. Tell me what's been happening."

"Where to start," mused Paul.

"At the beginning." Chuckled Athena.

"Hope you're ready for this." Paul began.

With that. Paul explained everything that had happened over the previous three months. Starting with Ewan stealing and him being arrested. Employing Belinda and having to buy a bigger van because of the products being sold.

"Sounds like it's been a bit of a roller coaster ride Paul!" gulped Athena.

"You could say that" agreed Paul. "It's certainly been a challenging time."

"Before we discuss anything else," interrupted Athena. "What are the numbers looking like Paul?"

This made Paul smile. "Well," smirked Paul. "This is the good bit. The team's absolutely smashing it and Belinda has been a revelation."

"What do you mean?" Athena shot back excitedly.

"To date. The store managers have carried out a hundred and forty-four assessments. Converting eighty-four of these into purchasing many of our other products. Increasing their average transaction value by 50% to seventy-five pounds."

"But that's only half the story. In tandem, they've also increased order frequency to once a month. Which increases the annual spend by a mind blowing 200%. From three hundred to nine hundred pounds for each customer every year."

"Belinda has picked up the baton very quickly. Making sure we're still signing up plenty of new business customers and home printing packages."

"In the first three months, she's picked up sixty new business customers and seventy-two home printing packages. As well as forming a fantastic bond with the team."

"Wonderful Paul." Enthused Athena. "Now it's about being consistent in our approach, with continuous reviews."

"I sense there's something wrong Paul," stopped Athena.

"Yes." Mumbled Paul. "The team are doing a magnificent job and the numbers and stats are fantastic." Paul left a long pause.

"But?" helped Athena.

"Very soon we're going to implode and grind to a halt." Warned Paul. "I've already had to get a bigger van, and that's on finance! We're selling products that are much bigger than we're geared up to handle."

"Each morning the stores are jammed with products to be delivered, and it's only going to be a matter of time before things spill onto the shop floor."

"We're having desks, chairs, cupboards, filing cabinets delivered, along with smaller stationery items, catering products and workplace solutions."

"There's not much room in a small shop, and as the team complete more assessments and win new customers. We're going to reach breaking point."

"I hear you Paul," confirmed Athena. "It's something I did expect to happen. But not so early in our business re-engineering project."

"Which is a good thing." Athena smiled. "And proves what an amazing job you're all doing. Well done."

"I must warn you though," she said, looking deep into Paul's eyes. "This next phase is going to be the most difficult and will either make or break the business."

Paul took a huge gulp. "What do you mean Athena."

"You need to close all three stores, streamline the business and relocate into a single business unit," answered Athena, adding, "I'm serious."

"Shit." Blurted out Paul. "Sorry I didn't mean to swear. I'm just shocked."

"Don't worry. I understand. This is huge Paul and the only way you can pull it off is through planning. Everything has to be nailed down tight," said Athena, a wild look raged in her eyes.

"Before we can plan anything, we need to work out when we can do it. But before we can even do this. You need to understand when your store leases end and start looking at prices and availability of business units."

"Location is very important Paul. Only look at areas with good motorway access, close to your current customer base and easy access for the team."

"How are we ever going to afford rent on a business unit Athena," Paul questioned defeatedly.

"You're not thinking straight Paul." Snapped back Athena. "How much are you paying in rent across the three stores?

"About eighteen hundred pounds a month," replied Paul.

"Well, I'd be surprised if we can't get a decent sized business unit for less," explained Athena, "We'll save on rates, electricity and water too!"

"That being said," qualified Athena. "There's going to be lots of other challenges for us to address along this part of the journey."

"We're going to need to move pretty fast on this Paul," hurried Athena. "We'll meet again next month. When I want you to have the store lease situation clear and a preferred business unit location in mind."

Paul didn't want to worry the team or take their mind off phase three activities. On workdays he carried on with bold calls and leafleting. In the evenings and at weekends he'd check the leases and view potential units.

The following month, he'd arranged to pick Athena up. They were on their way to view a business unit, and whilst they travelled discussed the leases.

"Paul. Where do we stand with the three leases?" Asked Athena.

"It turns out. After the original three-year lease had expired, we'd never been given new leases to sign at both Blackburn and Accrington," explained Paul. "They're owned by families, who'd just forgotten to get them renewed."

"It wasn't so simple with Rawtenstall. We still have twelve-months left. But after explaining, the landlords were very understanding, and will allow us to exit with three-month notice. On the understanding that we leave it as we found it."

"That's great." Nodded Athena. "We now have a timeline to work towards."

Paul turned into 'The Courtyard.' It was a small business park with twelve units in a U shape, with secure gates and room for parking and deliveries.

"They parked and Paul explained. "This location is bang in the middle of our customer base; Blackburn is eight miles to the left, Bury is ten miles to the right, Bolton is twelve miles behind us and Burnley is ten miles straight ahead."

"We're viewing unit six," Paul said pointing the way.

"It spans three thousand square feet, has a small reception, a small office and a showroom that just needs some electric to make it a perfect office for the team."

"There's masses of space for storage and work areas both upstairs and downstairs. It's a perfect location and has lots of room for us to expand."

"It sounds ideal, Paul. How much is it?" asked Athena.

"Compared to others it's a little more expensive. But the trade-off is the location and that we don't have to spend much to get operational. Including service charges and buildings insurance it's twelve hundred and fifty pounds a month."

"That's still a fair saving against the store leases," commented Athena. "Come on. Let's go look."

The agent opened-up, explained some operational things, before leaving them to have a good look round.

Athena didn't need much convincing. "It's perfect Paul. Let's get straight back to mine to look at potential moving dates and start planning."

Athena brewed the coffee, whilst Paul got out his laptop and made ready to start creating a planning spreadsheet.

Fresh coffee filled the air, Athena sat down next to Paul saying. "We're already in December Paul and you need to give a three-month notice, so that immediately takes us into March. I suggest we aim for Easter weekend."

"Good Friday falls on the 4th April and the long bank holiday weekend will provide four days to clear out the shops, transfer the stock and get set up."

"Which means you can close as normal on the Thursday night and open again as you normally would on the Tuesday morning. The only difference being location."

"I get that and even though it'll be tough. I can see it working," confirmed Paul. "But what about all those customers who come into the stores?"

"You've got to understand Paul, your business is changing and has to change if it's to survive. Stopping in stores forever is not an option," said Athena.

"I do understand." Replied Paul. "I'm worried these people won't order from us once we move, and we'll lose a significant amount of cash business."

Athena pondered for a while. "I've an idea: The eCommerce system you have. Why not add your own products to it, so current store customers can have options to pay over the phone or online and you'll deliver for free?"

"That's a good idea," Paul thought aloud. "Our phone system is cloud based so we can take it anywhere. As well as having a new freephone number, if customers carry on ringing the direct store numbers, they'll still work."

"If we couple this with putting all our products online and setting up an online payment terminal, which the team can use to take card payments over the phone, it should reduce the amount of store customers we lose."

"We'll have to advertise the hell out of it," continued Paul. "Ringing, writing and emailing every customer clearly explaining what's happening."

"I agree," stated Athena. "Let's think about those store customers some more. Normally, they're used to walking in, buying what they want and walking out again. We are now asking them to wait a day for a delivery."

"If we're not careful, those customers (not on a home printer package) could revert to going to the supermarket to get what they want quickly."

"You're right," agreed Paul, thinking some more. After a short pause. "We could provide same day delivery for any products we have in stock. We'd need to have a cut off though, say eleven in the morning, to allow for deliveries."

"Agreed again," said Athena. "This now brings us onto a more difficult question Paul." Athena was again looking deep into Paul's eyes.

"I fear this is something I'm not going to like Athena," whispered Paul.

"Probably not." She replied quietly. "But it's something that must happen to safeguard the future of the business."

"You better hit me with it then Athena," demanded Paul.

"The business is going to move from a reactional consumer business to a predominately proactive business to business organisation. No longer will you need team members to serve people walking through the door."

"We've already started the change process with the store managers, but the rest of the team members need to be willing to change too."

"No longer will they be able to hide behind a counter and wait for people to walk through the door, they're going to have to be proactive in some way."

"Belinda will be fine. She can carry on working from home. The store managers will need a little tweaking to become account managers."

"It's the likes of Tim, Steph and Adele, who are going to need to change the most. Chris is no problem; he can manage the warehouse and do most of the deliveries."

"But the others need to change and become customer service and technical personal, taking calls, solving technical issues and carrying out installations."

"Installations?" Questioned Paul.

"Definitely," confirmed Athena. "As we move forward, we'll be introducing business printing and other technical packages too, and in most instances an installation and onsite support services will be required."

"Bloody hell." Exclaimed Paul. "Sorry for the expletive. I wasn't expecting that in the middle of this move planning conversation."

"Sorry for dumping this on you Paul." Apologised Athena. "But it's better you know this now, so we can include this requirement in our plans too."

"My turn to agree, Athena," nodded Paul. "But I also think we've got enough skills in the team to cope for now, as long as they're willing to change."

"Steph is very technically minded and as well as taking phone orders and doing quotes, she's more than capable of providing first line support."

"And Tim has already done some installations for home customers who were willing to pay for someone to install their home printing package."

"Then there's Adele. Although reserved. I think she's perfect for customer services, as she's more comfortable talking on the phone than face to face."

"That's it all covered Paul," confirmed Athena. "Time for you to write up the project plan, discuss everything with the team, have those individual role change conversations, give notice on the leases and hold onto your hat."

"One last thing," added Athena. "Come moving weekend you are going to need the entire team to help you. It's a monumental task to undertake and will probably take three or four days to complete."

"You've got lots to plan Paul. But I'd like to meet with you again a week prior to the move, so we can be sure everything is ready. In the meantime, please keep everyone focused on phase three," finalised Athena.

Paul brought the team together one evening in their regular team meeting watering hole, the Whitaker Arms. Providing food and drinks as before.

"Thank you for coming," he began. "You've been doing a fantastic job and I wanted to tell you how proud I am and how much I appreciate you."

The team nodded back in approval.

"Although important. This isn't the main reason for bringing you together tonight." Silence ensued and all ears were pricked ready for listening.

"You've been doing such a great job the stores are bursting at the seams and struggling to cope with our new business model. If we don't change, one day soon it's all going to implode and come crashing down."

Don (Paul's confidant and the person the team listened to) piped up. "Totally agree Paul. It's getting harder each day with all the extra stuff, especially the furniture. What do you have in mind."

"It's time to close the stores and move into a business unit." Began Paul. "We'll have much more space, most of us will be together as one team and it'll provide us with masses of expansion capabilities."

"What about the walk-in customers?" asked Adele.

"We'll provide a free same day delivery service. Our telephone numbers will remain the same, although we'll also add a central freephone number. We'll also add our own products to the eCommerce website." Replied Paul.

"Where's the unit going to be located Paul." Asked Tim.

"It's on Grane Road in Haslingden." Started Paul. "We assessed both customer locations and your home locations, deciding Haslingden was the perfect place for everyone."

"When is it going to happen?" shouted out Steph.

"Easter weekend," confirmed Paul. "We'll close on the Thursday evening and reopen as normal on the Tuesday morning. Just in a different location."

The team seemed suitably impressed, looking at each other and nodding their heads with approval.

"Obviously, there's a lot of planning to do for the move," Paul Explained. "But let me worry about that. Please carry on concentrating on phase three."

"But. There is one very important thing I need your help with please: moving weekend. It's going to take a monumental effort to get it done."

"I know it's a bank holiday. But I can't do it without you. Of course. I'll pay you for your time and if we all muck in, we could have it done in three days."

Don committed immediately, with the other store managers following. It was a domino effect with the rest of the team agreeing one after the other.

Paul spent the following months planning for the move - It was very complicated. But he made sure he captured every activity in a detailed project plan, complete with timings and ownership responsibility.

It was the week before the move. Paul was on his way to see Athena. It had been December the last time Paul had seen Athena, he'd missed her.

Yes, there was certainly an underlying attraction for sure. But he missed Athena's help and guidance. Reassuring that he was doing the right things.

Paul constantly questioned his ability to lead. Was he doing it right? There's no blueprint to follow. Having Athena with him brought huge reassurance.

It was Spring. The sun was shining. The leaves on the trees were green, daffodils and crocuses stood to attention on the grass verge. Paul smiled.

His mind wandered; would Athena be in the back garden. 'Garden,' He thought. 'It was more like a forbidden hidden valley.'

Arriving he found the courtyard packed with fancy cars. He squeezed his (out of place Hyundai) into a small gap. Edged out of the partially open door (desperate not to touch an Aston Martin) and went to find Athena.

He rang the bell. There was no answer. Music was playing. It was coming from the garden. Paul decided to go for a look and headed round the back.

Stood in the same area as when he first witnessed the oasis and saw Athena training. His jaw dropped once again. But it wasn't the beauty of the garden.

Although it was truly beautiful. It was another scene before him that made his jaw drop. There were maybe thirty people (men and women) dressed in white robes, some with a sword on their back, others holding a long spear.

In the distance. He could see that the white tent was up and made out a dozen figures watching someone having a battle of some kind on the VR.

Paul spotted half a dozen people walking around the others wearing darker robes, holding large platters of fruit, meats, and goblets. Presumably, wine.

"Paul." Came a cry. "Paul over here." It was Athena. She was stood in a small group of people waving him over to join them.

Paul made his way across to the group. He felt way out of his depth. "Great to see you Athena. Have I come at a bad time?" He asked.

"Don't be silly Paul." Athena replied. "I've had this party booked in for ages and thought it'd be perfect to help lighten the weight on your shoulders."

"If I'd told you about it, there's no way you'd have agreed to come along today. Would you?" Athena asked.

"Probably not," Paul honestly replied.

"Do you remember, Paul?" Athena continued, "when you had a go on the VR, and I explained that I've a passion for ancient warfare and weaponry."

"Yes. That was an amazing experience." Paul smiled, remembering it fondly.

"Well. Each Spring I throw an ancient warfare garden party, inviting some close family and friends, who are also interested in the subject."

"This year. The theme is ancient Greece, hence the robes, swords, and spears. And as you can see. They ate lots of fruits, meats and drank wine."

"I'm hardly dressed for the occasion Athena" Laughed Paul. Looking down at his Khaki trousers and brown Karrimor walking boots.

Athena smiled. "Don't worry. I anticipated it."

She reached down, picked up a brown paper bag and handed it to Paul. Inside was a white robe, belt, and a pair of sandals. "Just pop in the house and change in the bathroom," winked Athena.

Paul blushed. He was embarrassed. But couldn't refuse Athena in front of her guests. He thanked her and made his way to the house.

Paul had a dilemma. He didn't know what to do with his undies. Should he remove them like the Scots do when wearing a kilt? Or should he leave them on and risk offending others but keep some dignity. He chose the latter.

Ten minutes later he reappeared and whispered his dilemma into Athena's ear. She let out a loud shriek of laughter saying, "you chose well Paul."

Paul had a wonderful time. Athena's guests were lovely people, rich in kindness and knowledge. The weight lifted from his shoulders for a time.

After Athena's last guests departed, they sat together in the garden to catch the last of the Spring sunshine.

Athena turned to Paul. "Today wasn't about checking your moving plans Paul. It's too late for that and I have trust, you'll have it all buttoned down."

"Today was about relieving some of the stress. This period has been your most intense to date. But these next three or four weeks will determine if we've still got a chance of completing the business transformation."

"I need you to be completely focused and ready to get the job done. To be pig headed, to persevere and drive the team to overcome every obstacle."

With that Athena took Paul in her arms, gave him a long loving hug, pecked him on the cheek and whispered, "we'll meet again in one month."

Chapter 10. Moving Day

It was four in the morning. Paul woke dripping in sweat. His mind was racing. What if this happened. What if we couldn't do that. Anxiety took hold.

For the next hour he lay with his eyes wide open. His mind racing a thousand miles an hour. There was no chance of getting anymore sleep.

He slipped out of bed, crept downstairs and had a long hot shower.

Still with hours to fill before the day really started. He decided to take his dog (Shadow) on an ultra-long walk. Which might just clear his thoughts.

Shadow was an English Springer Spaniel and named after the Springer in Michael Morpurgo's book 'Shadow.' And he was no different, always by Paul's side. The perfect shadow.

The walk did them both good. Shadow was content and laid on his bed. Paul had cleared his thoughts and formulated a clear plan, what was to happen over these next three or four days.

In the weeks prior, Paul had already got the unit as much ready as he could. Electrics and heating had been installed, desks and chairs were built. The warehouse racking was put together and ready in location.

They were using the same business system as already in the stores. Which was one less thing to worry about. Although, the three separate systems still had to be integrated into one and a new office network configured.

A stock control system would be part of the new solution: It was already available in the existing software. But they hadn't needed to use it before. In this new world though. They had to know what was available. Because they couldn't see it.

But. Before any of this could happen, the stock from all three stores had to come to the unit and be organised. And the stores had to be cleaned out from top to bottom.

The Rawtenstall store was going to cause the biggest obstacle; the Landlord insisted it must be left in the same condition we found it in. Even if that meant, it was in worse condition that it currently was. It didn't make sense.

Which meant stripping out the counter, getting rid of the flooring, ripping out the work benches and giving each room a lick of paint.

Luckily, the families who owned the other two stores were sensible and happy for him to leave them complete. They knew that the team had vastly improved the stores. But Paul still had to make sure that they were left clean and tidy.

Paul put together the work teams. Thursday night was bagging all the rubbish and getting together any spent electrical items from each store. Ready for multiple refuse centre trips the following morning.

Friday morning saw the work teams organise, box and label the stock. Whilst Paul traveled round and completed the refuse centre trips.

Friday afternoon, Paul traveled around each store and transported the stock to the unit, whilst the work teams cleaned down the stores.

At the same time. Steph (as the self-nominated IT department) got on with integrating the three systems, building the new network, and configuring the stock control system.

Saturday saw a change. Chris was given the important job of unpacking and organising the stock. Ready to add it to the stock control system once Steph had it configured.

The rest of the team high tailed to the Rawtenstall store to help with the deconstruction. Paul again acted as the refuse centre taxi. Transporting the wooden panels and flooring as it was made available.

On Sunday, the paint rollers broke out in force and by lunch time, the walls were covered as required. Leaving just Chris to finish populating the stock.

Paul had a final swing round the stores, bagging any remaining rubbish left behind. Before handing the keys back to the landlords.

Arriving back at the unit. He thanked everyone for the immense effort they'd put in and handed each a bottle of Prosecco to celebrate, reminding them that payment for their time will be added to their monthly salary.

He wished them well. Thanked them again. Both he and they were happy to have a little down time before they officially opened on Tuesday morning.

Paul had one last check round the unit. Making sure everything was ready for Tuesday. The IT systems were checked and working. The store telephone numbers transferred to their phone system. The freephone number was working. Stock could be checked, and the online payment system was ready.

Tuesday arrived. Everybody was a little early and full of anticipation. Paul was praying the systems they'd built and the thousands of customer letters and emails they'd sent, would secure much of their existing business.

Before the move Paul had sat down with each team member clearly explaining what would be required of them. Answering any concerns and providing each of them with a new job profile and contract.

The store managers were now account managers. Each had an allotted postcode area. Any business customers within these postcodes, were theirs to manage and grow through building strong relationships.

The mornings were put aside for calling their customers, doing quotations, and arranging assessments. Assessments were carried out in the afternoons.

Adele, Steph, and Tim formed the customer service team. Managing orders and queries that came in by phone and email or through the website.

Steph would also be first line support for any technical support issues and Tim would be on call to carry out any installations or onsite fault finding.

Chris was happy managing the warehouse, doing most of the deliveries and carrying out stock control.

As she worked from home, nothing really changed for Belinda, which she was very pleased about.

In those initial two – three weeks Paul paused the bold calling and leafleting, as he wanted to measure what was happening with orders, make sure the systems worked and the team were supported in what they were doing.

Business, schools, and printing package customers carried on as nothing had happened. Communication with these customers was traditionally by phone or email, so nothing changed, and transactions were at normal levels.

But Paul was worried. In The first week he'd seen a sharp decline in the old walk in customer business. Which still accounted for 40% of their business.

It was down by 50%. Meaning their overall revenues were down by 20%. This was a large amount of cash and meant they would be losing money.

Paul didn't know what to do. They'd communicated several times with all their customers. Building ordering systems and providing same day delivery. He'd even put posters at the stores, telling people to call for free delivery.

The same thing happened in week two and three. Paul was beside himself.

To support them with the move. Paul had negotiated a bank overdraft. But they were already eating into it and at this rate it wouldn't last long.

Chapter 11. It's All About Team

Paul was relieved. It was time to meet Athena. He needed someone to share the burden. Someone to talk to who'd understand, and who may be able to come up with some suggestions to help get through this.

The last thing he wanted to do at this delicate time was to worry his team with this problem. He needed them to have full focus on the task at hand and keep the orders coming in, if there is any chance of survival.

Athena opened the door to be greeted by a disheveled looking Paul. He was unshaven, with crumpled clothes and deep red eyes from crying.

He fell into Athena's arms. She held him tight, in a way that took him back to the time they first met. Warmly hugging him like his mother used to do.

"Paul whatever is the matter," expressed Athena. "You're so upset, and you look like you haven't slept for weeks."

Parting slightly, Paul looked deep into Athena's striking blue eyes. His lips quivering and legs shaking as he began to speak.

"The move went so well. The team was magnificent. Everything worked like a dream. Except," Paul hesitated.

"Except what? Athena questioned.

"The walk-in consumer business." Paul blurted out. "We've lost 50% of it. I thought it was just a blip. But it's been the same the whole three weeks."

"That translates into losing 20% of our overall revenue and will mean. If it carries on at the same rate. A five-thousand-pound loss every month, suffocating us."

"Pull yourself together Paul!" demanded Athena. "Come inside and we'll talk it through over coffee."

Athena brewed the coffee. Whilst Paul visited the downstairs bathroom to wash his face and compose himself. They reconvened at the meeting table.

"You need to be calm." Started Athena. "Don't let anxiety consume you. To analyse a situation to understand what's happening. You need a clear head."

"It's only when things become clear, can you find a solution to fix things."

"I take it, you've carried out everything detailed in the plan."

"Yes. Exactly as planned," Paul calmly explained. "Customer letters and emails were sent out on two occasions. Once before the move and again just after. I've also tested the eCommerce system again and it works well."

"Hmmm..." pondered Athena. "I expected we'd lose some of the walk-in business. But I thought maybe 10% or at the most 20%. Not 50%."

"Just goes to show some people just don't like change. I suspect the lost 50% will not change, wanting still to walk in somewhere to buy a cartridge. They're most likely now buying from the supermarket."

"Unfortunately. You're unlikely to change these habits. Unless you can convert these people onto your home printing package."

"Please tell me the numbers again Paul, including whatever cash reserves you have," Athena asked.

"Walk-in sales accounted for 40% of the overall business. Which means on the current trajectory we've lost 20% of revenues. When working this back to net profit. We'll lose about five thousand pounds a month."

"Before the move. I presented our plans to the bank and asked for their support, in the form of a thirty-thousand-pound overdraft, which they agreed to."

"Our other cash reserves were used to deck the unit out, ready for moving in. The way I see it, we've got six months left before it's lights out time."

"Hold on Paul," Athena interjected. "You're looking at this completely wrong. Your glass needs to be half full. Not half empty."

"What do you mean?" Questioned Paul.

"Instead of believing you've only got six months left in business. You should be saying you've got six months to turn the situation around."

"The quicker you can reduce the losses, the more time you buy. Let's say after three months the losses are two and half thousand pounds. That buys you another six months."

"I understand," confirmed Paul. "Are you saying that we can find a way out of this Athena?"

"Absolutely," she smiled. "Paul you've got to understand. What we've done is huge. Overnight we've closed three retail stores and opened a business to business technical services organisation."

"The retail business was having a heart attack and it was flatlining. We've jump started it, and got it going again. But it's going to take time to recover. When it does though, it'll be a completely different business."

"Don't get me wrong. We need to get back as much of the walk-in business as we can. But over time we must attract more business customers to lessen the reliance on consumer transactions."

"The business development structure we put in place before the move was working. You need to get back out bold calling and leafleting. Together with making sure the team understands the importance of hitting their targets."

"I don't want to burden the team with our dire financial situation. As I think it could have a real negative effect on their performance," worried Paul.

"On the contrary," disagreed Athena. "You must be honest and transparent with them. You'll be surprised by their reaction. In my experience. When backs are against the wall. Your team will dig in and do everything to help."

"Another thing," continued Athena. "Whilst you and Belinda are busy attracting new customers and the account managers are growing business in the existing business customers."

"Focus the customer service team on ringing the lost walk-in customers. To either convert them onto the home printer package or at least, win back some of the transactional cartridge business."

"I want to show you something Paul..." Athena rose and changed the conversation. "Come out into the garden with me."

The conversation with Athena allowed Paul to control his anxiety and look at the situation differently, certainly in a more positive way. He took the last mouthful of coffee and followed Athena out into the garden.

Athena took Paul by the hand and led him down deep into the garden. "Paul," she whispered. "There's something I've been hiding from you."

Paul looked at her confused. "What do you mean Athena."

"Remember I've told you about my passion, ancient warfare and weaponry." Asked Athena.

"Yes. I remember." Replied Paul.

"Well that's only part of the story," continued Athena. "As well as it being my passion. I'm highly trained in most global fighting styles. New and old."

"I could see that when watching you on the VR." Commented Paul.

"No Paul," corrected Athena. "That was purely exercise. When I say highly trained. I mean. To the point where when I was younger. I was employed to destroy dictators and their armies all over the world."

Paul wasn't sure what to say. He was stunned. "Don't worry Paul, I'd never hurt those close to me, which includes you," she reassured him.

"The reason I'm telling you this Paul," continued Athena. "Is that once my team had cleared societies of these bad people, we had to help them rebuild."

"Most of the time. This meant taking a few steps back before they could find their feet, stablising the situation, before progressing forward again."

"There were many times, we had to help shape new governments, build infrastructure and train people to lead, defend and care for communities."

"What I'm trying to do is put into perspective what you're facing. Yes, it's hard. But these communities faced seemingly insurmountable obstacles, and they, on most occasions, overcame adversity to succeed."

"Sometimes. As in this case. You need to take a step back and regroup. Before you can push on again and smash through the glass ceiling."

They stopped at a marble clad doorway, which seemed to lead into the belly of the hillside. Athena pushed open the heavy doors and the lights immediately flickered, revealing a cavernous room carved into the rock.

Paul felt a blast of heat and caught sight at the opposite side of the cavern, what could only be described as, a huge blacksmiths forge. Adorned on the walls were hundreds of different bladed weapons. All shapes and sizes.

Athena explained. "This is my secret and most favorite place in the whole world. It's my hide-away. A place I come when I want to forget everything. Forging ancient weapons takes me to a place where I'm at peace Paul."

Paul was gob smacked. He knew there was something very different about Athena. Something unique. Something which caused physical attraction.

But he'd never suspected she was some kind of assassin, who was paid to topple tyrants, and who had a weapon making factory in her back garden.

"I don't know what to say Athena." Began Paul. "This place is amazing. Is the weapon making connected to your time fighting dictators?" Paul couldn't believe he was asking this question. But left it hanging in the air anyway.

Athena didn't bat an eyelid. "It comes from a time way before. Back when my home was in Greece. This was when I'd travelled the world studying and learning ancient warfare and weaponry."

"Not just learning to fight. But learning to forge too. Being able to make faultless weapons was a revered skill back in ancient times. The Japanese were masters at this and produced some of the best swords in the world."

"Learning from the most revered weapon makers, the greatest fighters and the best war tacticians in the world, made me the person I am today."

"That's enough about me. I've brought you to my special place. Because I want to show you how something as faultless as a Samurai sword is made."

"Would you like to find out Paul?" questioned Athena.

Paul couldn't contain his excitement. He'd always wanted to visit Japan to understand more about Japanese culture. "Absolutely." Grinned Paul.

"Great." Responded Athena. "We'll have to change into protective clothes."

Athena led Paul to a smaller room off the main Cavern, which had a range of protective equipment hanging up. She picked him out a selection of items.

Athena slipped off her robe, revealing an exceptionally toned muscular body. Paul was embarrassed. His cheeks warmed with embarrassment.

She'd changed so much from when they'd first met. Although she seemed much older back then. She was still an attractive lady. But now. Her hair was jet black, skin silky smooth and she had the body of an Amazonian.

Paul couldn't help it. She'd mesmerized him. He stood in amazement. Wondering how he'd befriended such a beautiful and intelligent woman.

Athena had this effect on people. It's happened all her life. With Paul it was different. She respected him. He always controlled his feelings and never allowed it to consume him. She knew this was a great skill in her presence.

Athena released him from her spell. "Come on Paul. Follow me."

Paul followed Athena and they made their way over to the ranging forge.

"Before we start Paul." Directed Athena. "Time for a quick history lesson on the making of swords for the Samurai."

"The correct name for the sword is katana. But most people refer to it as a Samurai sword, as it's depicted this way in the modern media and movies."

"Katana's are traditionally made from a special Japanese steel called tamahagane. Which is created from a traditional smelting process to remove impurities and even out the carbon content of the steel."

"The smelting process takes four or five people a week to complete. Producing a steel bloom known as a kera. A single kera is worth hundreds of thousands."

Paul was clearly fascinated. So, Athena carried on.

"Tamahagane is then extracted from the kera and sold to master sword makers like me. And here's some layers of tamahagane we'll be using."

Athena began folding and welding pieces of the tamahagane several times, working out the differences. Drawing out the resulting block to form a billet.

She then coated the blade with several layers of a wet clay slurry. Shouting over to Paul. "This process is called tsuchinoko, the edge of the blade is coated with a thinner layer than the sides and spine."

Athena heated the sword and quenched it in water. Telling Paul. "The slurry causes only the blade's edge to be hardened and makes the blade curve, due to the difference in densities of the micro-structures in the steel."

"Now the blade is forged," Athena proudly announced, holding it high above her head. "Although it's not polished up yet. Would you like to have a feel?"

"Yes please," grinned Paul.

Athena handed over the Katana. Although no handle yet. Paul was amazed how light and balanced it felt and imagined being a Samurai for a second.

"I feel privileged Athena. Thank you," confessed Paul, whilst handing the blade back to Athena. "What happens to it now?"

"I'll send it off to my polisher," announced Athena. "The polishing process can take three weeks. They use a series of successively finer stones in a process called glazing. They'll also add a handle and a scabbard (sheath)."

Come on, let's get changed and have a wrap up back at the house. Paul knew what was coming, so he looked the other way and waited for Athena to be clothed before turning around. Athena smiled to herself knowingly.

Back at the house Athena spoke. "I'm glad you enjoyed making the katana Paul. But there is a serious side to why I wanted you to experience it."

"Making a katana. Is not like making any other sword. Most other swords can be completed in a few hours. A katana can take many months."

"I liken it to building a winning team. Which is not an easy thing to do."

"It can take years to form a team with the same shared values, who look out for one another and have the companies and customers interests at heart."

"A katana starts way back in the smelting process when four or five people constantly work on the shared goal and process of producing a kera."

"A kera provides tamahagane to the sword maker, which he forges, welds, and folds as many as sixteen times before the impurities are removed."

"The process continues. With the polisher taking up to three weeks to remove the roughness, making it gleam and smooth, with a razor-sharp edge."

"Don't doubt what it takes to make a winning team Paul. As we go through this process. It's likely some of your team will decide it's not for them."

"You've taken them to a different world. A world they're not used to. Some will adapt and change, flourish even. Others will just not want to."

"I liken people to icebergs," smiled Athena.

"How does that work?" Questioned Paul. Who'd been listening intently.

"Only 10% of an iceberg sticks out of the water. The other 90% you can't see, is below the water line." Explained Athena.

"That's just like people. What they want you to see. The stuff you can see and hear, adds up to just 10% of their identity. The other 90% is hidden somewhere inside."

"And one of the hardest things to do. Is to try and change a person's identity. Especially if they don't want to change."

"Our business transformation project will take some of your team way out of their comfort zone, forcing them to make a choice. Do I want to change identity or not? Some will and some won't."

"All you can do Paul. Is to act as the facilitator. Help them understand what's required. Train them where they need training and if all else fails. Help them exit the business to find something they're comfortable doing."

"Wow," exhaled Paul. "I wasn't expecting a learning so deep connected to making a sword for a Samurai."

"I understand and I know it's going to be a challenge for both them and I. It's new for us all. Coming from small teams in a reactive environment, to being all together and asked to behave in a completely different proactive way."

"This is going to be your next challenge Paul. It's critical that you get the team onside and doing their new jobs fast, if the business is to succeed."

Athena continued. "The next three months are critical, and we've got to put a big dent into the current losses. This can only be achieved with all the team being focused on proactivity and on the activities we discussed early."

"You've also got to be transparent and honest with them. Get them together. Lay it on the line. If things don't turn around quickly everyone's out of a job. Including you. But also explain how they can help fix it."

"Okay. Got it Athena," confirmed Paul. "When do you want to meet next?"

"It needs to be three months, as it's the critical time-line. And we'll either have a drink to celebrate or commiserate." Athena half joked.

Monday Paul called the team together in the main office, even asking Belinda to join them for an hour. He thought it best everyone was involved.

"Thank you everyone for attending." Paul nervously began. "Moving weekend went perfectly, and you guys were simply fantastic. Thank you."

"That being said. We have a real problem. Which I need your help to fix."

Paul laid it on the line. "We've lost 50% of the store walk in business. Which equates to 20% of our overall revenues, and we are on course to lose five thousand pound every month. And if we don't fix it fast, we're all out of a job in six months."

Paul looked around the room. There was shock written across their faces, some couldn't bear to look at Paul, looking at their shoes instead.

It was Don who spoke up. "Less than an ideal situation Paul. I'm sure you're worried to death. Thank you for being honest with us about the situation."

"You said. If we don't fix it fast. Which to me means that you've got an idea of how the situation could be fixed. What do you need us to do?"

The rest of the team looked on and listened intently.

"As a team the activities we were doing before the move were working," explained Paul. "We need to double down and do more of them, and I need to get back out bold calling and leafleting too."

"In addition, Tim, Steph, and Adele, at every spare opportunity, need to call the lost walk-in customers. To either convert them onto the home printer package or at least, win back some of the transactional cartridge business."

"If we can reduce the losses down to two and half thousand in the first three months it buys us another six months. That should give us enough time to rectify things."

"That sounds do-able," suggested Don. Most of us need to concentrate on what we've been doing but doubling down and doing more of it."

"Tim, Steph and Adele it's really you guys who's going to be required to do some things you've never really done before. How do you feel about this?"

The three of them looked at each other and nodded. Steph spoke up for them. "This is something we may be uncomfortable doing. But it's something we must do for the good of the business and team. We're all in."

Paul felt proud. He even had to wipe a tear or two away. The team had a group hug and promised each other, they'd do everything in their power to turn this situation around.

Chapter 12. Predicting the Future

Three months had passed, and Paul was in a much brighter place. The team over delivered against their promises. Losses were down to two thousand a month, and it was only a matter of time before they were back on an even keel.

Athena made good on her promise too. Which was to celebrate or commiserate (Paul was pleased it wasn't the latter.) She'd arranged to meet Paul in Manchester, at her favorite Greek restaurant, where she'd booked a private booth.

Athena has been eating at Kosmos for 40 years since it first opened. The excellent, traditional Greek and Cypriot food make her feel right at home.

Owner Loulla was born in a small traditional village in Cyprus. Learning all about generations-old Cypriot and Greek cuisine from her grandmother.

Paul was beaming by the time he sat down beside Athena. "This looks like a wonderful place Athena, thank you for inviting me along."

"It reminds me so much of home," smiled Athena. "I come here at least twice a year. Sometimes more if I can't get back to Greece for a while."

"I hope you don't mind. Loulla does a fantastic tasting menu. So, I've taken the liberty of pre-ordering, as I'd like you to experience many different dishes."

"Hey, I'm not complaining, as you're paying. You're entitled to order anything you want," laughed Paul.

"Whilst we're waiting for the food to arrive, why don't you fill me in on the figures?" Suggested Athena.

"Well," began Paul. "Today is exactly three months since we last met. When I made a complete idiot of myself. Weeping like it was the world's end."

"Paul, don't think like that." Countered Athena. "You've put your heart and soul into building this business, and you have a huge financial and personal investment in supporting your team. So, it was understandable."

"It's much appreciated you don't think less of me Athena," admitted Paul.

"On the contrary Paul," replied Athena. "I think more of you. It takes a lot of courage to emotionally show your feelings like you did."

Paul was blushing and quickly continued. "I took your advice. I was honest and laid it on the line with the team. Their response was magnificent."

"They've worked like trojans to turn the situation around. I think we'll be breaking even in another four months."

"That's wonderful news Paul," reassured Athena. "Which means we can now start to discuss and plan phase four."

"That's not what I expected today," admitted Paul.

Athena smiled. "It's okay to celebrate Paul. But it's not okay to stop and rest on your laurels. There's still much work to do before you truly reach safety."

"I agree," Paul mumbled. "After all, we're not even at break-even yet."

"Exactly," confirmed Athena. "Phase four is about shaping the future."

"What do you mean?" asked Paul.

"Many months ago. Remember when we first mapped out what the business needed to look like ten years from now?" questioned Athena.

"Yes, I remember. Like a mini IBM. Being the leading provider of office technology solutions to small and medium enterprises," answered Paul.

"More than that, Paul," added Athena. "We're going to disrupt the market with the products and payment solutions you develop and provide."

"Taking IBM's enterprise strategy, repackaging it and delivering it with honesty and transparency to SME's in affordable subscriptions."

"Exactly," agreed Paul. "With a vision to make office technology solutions affordable for all."

"Today," stated Athena. "We must plan out the first steps along this path."

"Ah, great timing," Loulla arrived with the most amazing array of Greek and Cypriot dishes. Athena and Paul tucked straight in.

There was taramasalata, olives, dolmades, moussaka, grilled meats, fresh fish, kleftiko, feta with other cheeses and a selection of baklava for dessert.

Once their appetite was quenched, Athena started the conversation again. "It's time to expand the services we are providing to SME's Paul."

"But the services have to help us move towards our vision. Initially, my suggestion is to build on the home printing package and develop a similar package for small organisations, including school classrooms."

"These organisations print much more than homes and will need extra functions like speed, multiple scanning, duplex printing and A3 options."

"Just like we did for the home package. It's about disruption Paul. Providing unlimited document printing for a guaranteed fixed monthly subscription. Which will save a good deal of cash against their current annual spend."

"Where this differs is in support. Together with phone support, you need a guaranteed onsite response. SME's can't afford to be without their printer technology for long. They need this certainty to gain total peace of mind."

"The future for all services is world class customer service with guaranteed affordable fixed prices. We need to be ahead of the curve."

"A small organisation print service." Announced Paul. "It's a great starting point Athena, one the team will be excited about, I'm sure."

"I'm assuming we'll promote it through the account manager assessments and through my bold calling activities?" Questioned Paul.

"Exactly," confirmed Athena. "I think it's probably time to develop a new corporate website too, that showcases our new products and tells our story."

"I know it's not something you can afford to outsource at this time. Do you think it's something Steph could put together with support from the team?"

"Steph's got some great IT skills and has been helping Tim out with designing the leaflets and handouts we've needed," confirmed Paul. "It'll be a challenge. But one I think she'll really enjoy and is capable of doing."

"That settles it then." Announced Athena. "We're into August already and there's only four months of the year left."

"Let's use this time to get into profitability, develop and roll out the small organisation printer technology service and build a new corporate website."

"We'll meet again early January. During this time, you must keep the pressure on the team. And carry out the weekly reviews, to make sure they are all delivering against their key performance indicators (KPI's)"

"Remember Paul. Your role is to support, train and facilitate. Don't be surprised if one or two decide change is not for them." Warned Athena.

Loulla cleared a space at the far end of the room and brought out three stools and microphones. Getting the place ready for some traditional Greek and Cypriot music.

Athena and Paul shared a bottle of a very tasty Greek red wine, whilst the music played.

The band started to play a tune that Athena adored. She jumped to her feet, dragged Paul to the small dance floor, and taught him the Hasapiko.

They'd had a great night. But it was time to leave, as the last night bus to Haslingden left Manchester at 11pm.

Not sure if you've ever been on the last X41 leaving Manchester on a Saturday night? It runs all the way through to Accrington and is like travelling on an 18 – 30's tour bus in Ayia Napa.

Everybody seems to have had a good time, some more so than others. Many asleep. Others canoodling and one or two emptying the contents of their stomachs.

Athena and Paul didn't speak much as they travelled. Instead they people watched. Smiling and laughing at the scenes unfolding before their eyes.

Paul was relieved when they arrived in Haslingden and hurried Athena off the bus, embarrassed how binge drinking is ingrained in our culture.

Athena assured him. "Paul it's the same in most places around the world. It might not be displayed the same. But it shows itself in many other ways."

"We were all young once and I'm sure we did some daft things we regret. But life's about learning and the older you get the wiser you should become."

Athena always managed to say the right things at the right time. She was truly blessed with great wisdom, amongst many other unique skills.

They arrived at the taxi rank. Paul gave the driver Athena's address, whilst paying him. They had a final hug of the year. Wished each other the best and departed into the night.

Monday morning Paul gathered the team and explained the plan to develop a small organisation and school classroom printer technology service, whilst also building a new corporate website.

The team was excited. As before. They all wanted to be involved with its development. Tasks were allocated and they agreed to reconvene the following week.

Paul and Steph met alone. To map out the bones of the new website. Paul could see Steph was excited and up from the challenge.

"Steph." Paul began. "All I want to do this morning is for us to agree on the main structure of the website. Following which. I want you to take ownership and use your creative skills. Involving the team where they're needed."

"That's great Paul," responded Steph. "I'm well up for it. But, please understand I have my main job to do first and foremost. So, developing the website will be a work in progress and take some time."

"Yes. I understand," agreed Paul. "What I would suggest, is to put the last two hours aside each day to work on the website. If the day job eats into this so be it but do your best to stick to the time plan."

"We've got about sixteen weeks to the end of the year and I'd like to see it completed by this time. This potentially gives you up to a hundred and sixty hours to completion. Do you think the time-line is fair?"

"More than fair." Agreed Steph. "Even allowing for the day job to eat into half the time. It will still give me enough time to complete the website."

For the next couple of hours Paul and Steph mapped out the new site. It had to look professional and be easy to understand, with no waffle.

They developed three main messages. We're simple to deal with. We're honest and trustworthy. We'll provide you with world class service. Which created their very own tagline. Simple Honest Service.

The following week the team reconvened. Paul had researched the SME market to understand their behaviour and work out their spend in this area.

"Our target market is clearly small organisations and primary school classrooms," Paul began confidently.

"Medium sized organisations require more expensive, faster, more robust and feature rich technology than what we'll be providing in our solution."

"On average small organisations and primary school classrooms use a set of printer cartridges every month. Spending around six hundred pounds annually."

"An interesting fact I found due to wanting to save money, most bought printers that aren't really up to the job and schools ended up replacing them every eighteen months or so, incurring additional cost."

"Like with the home printing package. The same principle applies with small organisations. "If we can reduce their annual spend by 50% and improve the service they're currently experiencing, we have a winning solution."

"Meaning, we have to provide a fit for purpose, wireless business multifunction inkjet printer with unlimited cartridges.

Which is supported by a next business day maintenance package for around twenty-five pounds a month."

Don jumped in. "That's good news Paul. We've been looking at Canon and Brother. Both have machines which are fit for purpose and within budget."

"The Canon machine is a little more cost effective for us. But the Brother can also print A3 in small volumes, providing extra functionality."

"Brother also have a couple of bigger machines that offer volume A3 printing, scanning, and copying too. They do cost more. But if anyone wants one, we could just increase the monthly price accordingly."

"Great work." Paul beamed. "Makes sense to go with the Canon as the main unit and keep the Brother as an option for occasional A3 printing requests. We've got the bigger machines in the kit bag for when they're needed."

"Best get one of each ordered in Don and put them through their paces for a week, to make sure they really are fit for purpose."

"It will also give Tim a chance to understand the technology and do a bit of training on them. As we'll be providing chargeable installations and an onsite repair or replacement service as part of the package."

Don ordered the machines and for the next week he and Tim put them through their paces, reporting the information back to Paul.

"Paul!!" Don shouted to get his attention. "Testing and training has been completed."

"What's the results?" asked Paul.

"Both decent machines and fit for purpose," Replied Don. "The Canon has slightly better print quality, but the Brother has the occasional A3 feature."

"Great!" Yelped Paul: "Time to get selling."

"Steph please can you develop some sales material for both the account managers and I to hand out. Make sure it gets added to the new website as an ecommerce page. Same as we agreed for the home package."

For the next four months the team doubled down and focused hard. By the end of the year they'd edged into profitability, and the small organisation printing package (which they'd called MY Print Service) was selling well.

Chapter 13. Building

As Athena had asked. Paul had been relentless with the account manager reviews, making sure they carried out enough assessments, followed up opportunities and made enough calls to close their opportunities.

Don was flying and didn't need much managing. Unsurprisingly, his administration was all over the place, but his numbers and conversations made up for it.

Harry and Barry were struggling a bit though. Paul was constantly on their case, about booking the right number of assessments and following up the opportunities that they produced.

There seemed to be different issues. Paul knew Harry was more than capable. He was a little lazy and liked to blame other factors as to why he hadn't done things, rather than take personal responsibility.

Barry though was different. He was much more reserved and would rather hide in the background. Barry was becoming much more of a challenge. Paul did his best with training and advice, but Barry was going backwards.

The final straw came one Monday morning. Barry came into work stinking of alcohol and slurring his words. Paul was convinced he was under the influence and wanted to send him home.

Barry protested his innocence, in a less than professional manner. It was only Don's interjection which calmed the situation, suggesting Barry best go and sort himself out. But the damage was well and truly done.

Only a matter of days had passed, and Barry asked to see Paul. Barry was clearly nervous and had something serious to discuss. Paul welcomed him into his office; "What's up Barry."

"It's time for me to move on Paul," explained Barry nervously. "I really appreciate the opportunity you have given me. But it's just not me."

"I'm not like Don or Harry who find it much easier to get along with people. I need a couple of drinks inside me before I can speak to people openly."

"Look. I'm sorry about the incident the other day. But that just sums things up. I stopped in the pub too long on Sunday night, because I couldn't face coming in to work on Monday morning."

"It's nothing to do with you or the rest of the team. Everybody has been extremely supportive and really helped me to try and make it work. But I'm kidding myself, I'm just not cut out for this type of work."

"Barry. I really appreciate your honesty," consoled Paul. "And don't worry I won't hold anything against you. I've known you for years and I respect you. Especially for having the courage to do this. What are you going to do?"

"I've decided to retrain as an engineer," answered Barry. "I'm good with my hands and love tinkering and fixing things." I'll earn less money, but it'll make me happy, as I'm getting more miserable by the day doing this."

"That's fair enough Barry and good on you," congratulated Paul. "Obviously, you've got a month's notice to work. And I'd really appreciate it if you'd make sure a professional handover happens over this period."

"Absolutely," confirmed Barry. "Thank you for being so understanding."

Paul followed Barry over to the main office and announced the sad news to the rest of the team. And asked Don and Harry to join him over in his office.

"Obviously. We're disappointed Barry is leaving" Began Don. "But that presents an opportunity for you two guys."

"What do you mean?" Questioned Don.

"Well," continued Paul. "We won't be bringing in anybody to replace him, as realistically two good account managers are more than enough to develop our existing customer base."

"But that means more work for us." Moaned Harry.

"Not sure how you've worked that one out Harry," said a quizzical looking Paul. "You'll still be working the same number of hours, doing the same amount of expected assessments."

"All that changes is that you have a larger customer base who will be placing more orders with you."

"So... Does that mean our targets go up too?" questioned Don.

"Unfortunately, it does," confirmed Paul "Splitting Barry's customers between the two of you, will also attract the same share of his target."

"That seems a little unfair Paul," quizzed Harry.

"Ah. But there is a silver lining for you guys," grinned Paul. "You also get to share his bonus structure too."

"The amount of bonus you can both earn by hitting target will increase by 50%." Paul was hoping this would do the trick and motivate Harry to take personal responsibility for his actions, to show his true capability.

Don looked at Harry saying. "I'm well up for this Harry. What about you?"

Don was confident in his capabilities and knew he could get much more out of Barry's customers than Barry had ever managed.

Harry hesitated. He knew if he'd put the effort in, he'd make some good money. But was he willing to commit and work that hard? Eventually he spoke; "Right. I'm in and I promise to give it my best shot."

"That's great. I'm really pleased you've both committed," smiled Paul. "Barry will be with us until Christmas and has promised to work with you to provide a professional hand over. Come January it's all yours."

True to his word Barry provided a great hand over to Don and Harry and introduced them to all his key clients.

The Christmas break was upon them, Paul and the team went out for a farewell drink with Barry. As the night ended, they wished each other well and went their separate ways, until after the new year.

Paul loved Christmas day. They were up early to watch the kids open their presents, basking in the delight they saw on their faces.

Late morning Paul began preparing dinner, ready for the in-laws arriving. Paul loved putting on a grand spread and overfeeding everybody.

They sat down to eat around five and the Prosecco started to flow. Paul was just about to tuck in when something came across him, he was delirious, everything felt like he was dreaming.

The next thing he remembered was waking on the cold wood floor and the family screaming around him. He couldn't breath and was choking.

With what seemed the last bit of life left in his body. Paul raised himself off the floor and sprinted towards the front door. Bursting outside he opened his lungs gasping for breath. His throat was burning white hot.

Paul's family followed fast behind. "Paul." They cried. "Are you okay? We thought you were dead. You collapsed and spasmed on the floor. Falling silent for what seemed an age. Before bursting into life again."

"I'm okay." Paul reassured them. "I don't know what happened. I just blacked out. My throat feels like it's on fire. My head seems foggy and my vision blurred. I feel utterly exhausted.

On Boxing day Paul travelled to the local medical centre to get checked out. They had a skeleton crew in, but luckily it wasn't busy. The doctor on duty turned out to be a parent from the children's primary school.

"What happened Paul?" He asked.

Paul explained yesterday's events. From blacking out at the table, spasming on the floor, not breathing, before bursting into life and running outside.

He listened intently and then asked. "How do you feel now?"

"Besides a huge bruise on the side of my head from the fall, my head feels full of fog. My vision seems blurred and I'm utterly exhausted," said Paul.

"I don't think it's heart related Paul, as everything checks out," diagnosed the doctor. "But I can't be sure. So, I'm going to ring ahead and book you an urgent checkup at Blackburn Infirmary. Set off over and they'll be waiting."

Paul entered the cardiology department, gave his details, and took a seat. It didn't take long before he was laid out and hooked up to various devices.

After many tests and five hours, a consultant came to see Paul. "Hello. It's good news. Your heart's in very good shape. But your ongoing symptoms suggest something else is wrong. So, I'm going to refer you to your GP for further investigation."

Paul rested up for what remained of the holidays, hoping his head and vision would clear before his return to work. Unfortunately, this didn't happen.

Arriving at the unit on the first day back after the holidays. Paul felt dreadful. He was exhausted. Dizzy. With seemingly slight blurred vision.

He gathered the team together and explained what had happened. "Now I just feel exhausted and like I'm in a constant dream." He continued.

"I'll need to rely on you all more than ever during this time, as I'll not be able to do half the things I would normally for the moment."

The team were really concerned and for a person committed to doing everything they could to keep the business moving forward.

Paul thanked them, gathered his things, and set off to meet Athena for their first session of the new year.

It was a very cold January morning. Frost was formed on the grass and icicles hung from Athena's front porch.

Paul just couldn't shake off his tiredness and dream-like state. Athena spotted him through the window and opened the door calling after him. "Paul, are feeling okay? You don't seem yourself."

He looked over. Athena looked even more beautiful in his dream-like state, her face unblemished and clear in the middle of his hazy world.

"Oh Athena," he began. "Where do I start?"

"Come in out of the cold," suggested Athena. "I've got fresh coffee brewed. You can tell me all about it, whilst we have a cup."

Paul followed her into the house, sat down and began pouring his heart out. Telling her everything that had happened, he explained Barry was leaving and detailing his fears of not being able to keep all the plates spinning.

Athena listened intently. Let Paul finish and gave him one of her special hugs, telling him that everything will work out and she'll make sure of it.

Paul wasn't sure what Athena could do in this situation. Indeed, she was a very special person, but he couldn't see how she could help his medical condition. Although he appreciated the hug, she gave great hugs.

"Before we talk about how we can help you," started Athena. "Tell me about the new small organisation print service and numbers please Paul."

A smile appeared. "The new print service is going well. The team did another fantastic job bringing it all together. It gave us an extra push towards the end of the year and December was our first profitable month."

"That's wonderful news," clapped Athena. "So, why's Barry leaving?"

"He's given up Athena and accepts the job role is just not for him," explained Paul. "The review process highlighted he was struggling."

"Both the team and I gave him our support with training and advice. But his heart wasn't in it. Even turning up for work once, he seemed under the influence of alcohol because the pressure was getting too much."

"Listen though, I'm not angry. I respect him more than ever for having the courage to come to terms with the situation and to do the right thing."

"So, how've you rearranged things?" Questioned Athena.

"Don and Harry have agreed to take on Paul's customers and target, as long as they also get his bonus too," confirmed Paul.

"That seems fair Paul." Agreed Athena.

"With Barry leaving the other two taking on his customers and target, it provides an opportunity to bring someone in to support you Paul."

"It's a little earlier than I had planned. But given your health situation, we have no choice. It's time you brought in a general manager to run the day to day operation. Allowing you to concentrate on strategy and development."

Paul gulped. "How are we going to afford that?"

"That's the easy bit," smiled Athena. "You can throw Barry's salary into the pot. The rest will come from the profits you have started to generate and efficiency savings the new manager will find."

"You sure about this Athena?" questioned Paul.

"Absolutely," confirmed Athena.

"The difficulty is finding the right person, who will bond with the team."

"You see Paul..." explained Athena. "It's a fine balance."

"You need someone who's going to (don't take this the wrong way) take the team to the next level. Which will require some team disruption, but at the same time, someone who the team will also embrace and welcome into the fold."

"It's quite a unique individual we need, and they are out there. But to attract the right type of person it's going to require a unique approach."

"What do you have in mind?" quizzed Paul.

"Time is of the essence too: Given your condition." Suggested Athena.

"Meaning, we need to weed out unsuitable people quickly and we don't have any available budget to work with recruitment consultants."

"So, we'll have to do this ourselves."

"Paul. Please write these instructions down and follow them to the letter," commanded Athena.

"First. Write a job advert that says:"

'Do you have ambition?

Can you build great teams?

Have you a strong track record of getting the best out of people?

Can you develop and build company-wide processes and procedures?

Are you ready for the challenge of taking a business to its next level?

Are you interested in earning over £30K a year?

Are you also friendly, enthusiastic, intelligent, self-motivated, driven, but most of all hungry to learn and advance your management skills?

Have you got high standards? But are you also courteous, mature and a team player when required?

Right now. We're looking for a once in a lifetime, dynamic and self-motivated general manager, who's keen to learn more. But already has unique skills of their own to help our company grow to its next level.

Working here will be a wonderful, lasting opportunity, that will challenge you, but also excite you and, if you are successful, will reward you.

If you answered yes to all the questions listed above. And believe this is you. Be ready to show us why when you call us today on XXXX XXXXXXX.'

"Then," Athena continued. "Post the job advert as an article on your website and across all your social media channels."

"There are also a number of free web-based job posting sites available. Indeed, is one. Just Google the others and list it on them too."

"Before you post it though. Buy a cheap pay as you go mobile and insert its number at the end of the advert. Then record this voicemail message on it."

'Good day. Thank you for your interest in joining our organisation.

In the first instance, after the tone please tell me your name, your mobile phone number, a little about yourself and explain why we should consider choosing you as our new general manager.

Then. If successful. We'll contact you to arrange a telephone interview. Wishing you all good things. Paul.'

"What this will do." Explained Athena. "Will immediately weed out any people who don't have the necessary skills. But also highlight the good ones. As they'll be the ones who'll plan what to say and leave a great message."

"Wow. I'd never have thought of doing it this way," admitted Paul.

"We've got to move fast Paul," hurried Athena. "So. Go get all that in place and done today and we'll meet back in two weeks to assess the replies and plan the next stage."

Two weeks passed and Paul was back with Athena. "How's the diagnosis going," asked a concerned looking Athena.

"In the last couple of weeks, I've seen that many specialists for this and that, I've actually lost count," laughed Paul. "They turned nothing up, and in the end the Doc has ruled everything out except chronic fatigue syndrome."

"What's that?" Questioned Athena.

"It's a form of Mental Exhaustion (M.E.)," explained Paul. "He used an analogy of a car's battery to explain what had happened."

"When a car is in constant use: Lights, Radio on, Devices charging and motor running. It uses a lot of energy and runs down the battery. But, If the battery is in good shape the car can recharge it quickly, whilst on the move."

"Although. If the battery is damaged it can't charge quickly. If it's overused, it will drain completely. Leaving the car with a flat battery."

"Basically. I have a damaged battery. Unfortunately, it's not something that can be replaced. On Christmas day my battery completely ran out."

"What does that mean moving forward Paul?" Quizzed Athena.

"I have to manage my time and not overexert myself. Any high energy activities have had to stop, and I've replaced them with dog walking."

"This is with me for the rest of my life. But if it's managed correctly, I'll be okay. My battery just takes much longer to charge than other people, and both heavy mental and physical activities drain it very quickly."

"I understand," confirmed Athena. "Which makes it critical that we quickly find the right general manager to take some of the pressure away from you."

"Agreed," said Paul.

Six people had left voicemails and four of them sounded ideal. Athena mapped out the next stage.

"Paul. I want you to text the unsuccessful ones to let them know, and thank them for applying"

"Then I want you to text the remaining four with a date and time for a telephone interview. You'll be asking them three questions, before deciding whether to bring them in for an interview and to meet the team."

"That sounds pretty straight forward," confirmed Paul. "What questions would you like me to ask them?"

"I want you to create an answers sheet for each person, which you need to fill in as they are answering these questions:"

What is your greatest business success and why?

What is your greatest business challenge and how did you overcome it?

What were your last three jobs and what did you like and dislike about them?

"Once each sheet has been completed. Please let the person know we are telephone interviewing four people and will contact them within the week if they've been successful and made it to the physical interview stage."

"You should be able to get this all done quite quickly. So. Let's meet next week to go through the answers and choose the people to interview."

The following week Paul and Athena got back together to go through the telephone interview questionnaires. "Who do you like?" asked Athena.

"I think the strongest are Pauline and Jackie. Both of which answered confidently without any hesitation on all three questions. Pauline has more experience. But Jackie just seems more dynamic and much more fun."

"I concur," agreed Athena.

"What next then?" questioned Paul.

"Invite them in for an interview," said Athena. "Both these ladies seem ideal. It's about seeing the whites of their eyes and getting to know them on a personal level and introducing them to the team."

"The team needs to be involved in the decision-making and feel they've made the final choice. They will then take ownership and make it work."

"Let the ladies know you'll be asking them a number of questions so you can get to know them a little better. And to prepare a small biography to deliver to the team, as they will be involved in the decision-making process."

"Your questions simply need to let you understand their family lives. Their partners and children (if they have any). What drives them on personally."

"Your final question is to ask for the name and contact details for their last three employers, which they detailed in the telephone interview. This will allow us to ensure they've done what they say and are trustworthy people."

"The team needs to play their part too. After the biographies. Plant a few questions for the team to ask. But make sure they ask each person the same questions. With the last one. To say something odd about themselves."

"Both interviews need to happen on the same day. Once complete tell the ladies you will call them either way inside a week, and then have a debrief with your team and let them choose who they want as their manager."

The following day, Paul called Pauline and Jackie and arranged for them to come for an interview later in the week and prepped the team accordingly.

Pauline was first. She was bright and bubbly. Maybe in her fifties. She'd been married for years and her kids had already left home. She had vast experience, was a lovely lady, and happy to provide reference contacts.

The team seemed to like her too. Pauline was very confident and delivered her biography with the help of some cue cards. The questions came and went, with the team finding out that Pauline loved keeping chickens.

An hour later it was time to welcome Jackie. This was a totally different experience. Jackie was much younger and in her mid-thirties. Married with two very young boys.

Although. Not as experienced as Pauline. She'd worked her way up in a finance business from a trainee to a regional manager. With full profit and loss (P&L) responsibility for many retail outlets, including team members.

Jackie had her first boy and was due back at work, to discover their second was on the way. After taking time out. Jackie was ready to progress back in management. But a little closer to home, to spend more time with her boys.

Paul immediately liked Jackie. He could see she was very determined and ambitious. She clearly had a caring side but wouldn't hesitate to address issues that stopped her from achieving her own or the company's aims.

Jackie took a different approach with the team. She didn't use cue cards. She was much more natural, and her nerves shone through in a good way, making them howl with laughter about her phobia of the humble tomato.

After Paul had shown Jackie out, thanking her for her time. He went for an immediate debrief with the team. 'So. What do you think then?"

Don piped up first. "I liked them both. But I think Jackie is much more on our wavelength. Probably helps that she's a good bit younger too."

Harry was next. "Yes. I agree with Don. Jackie hands down for me."

The rest of the team were nodding in approval. "Let's have a team vote." Suggest Paul. "Those who prefer Jackie raise your hands." It was unanimous.

The very next morning Paul rang Pauline and gave her the bad news. She was very disappointed as she really wanted the job. She was professional and thanked Paul for giving her the opportunity with the team.

Paul then rang Jackie. Giving her the good news and asking when she could start. Jackie was over the moon and told Paul it was a bonkers employment process, but she loved it. As she'd no current job, she'd start next Monday.

Before Jackie started, Paul wanted to see Athena to tell her the news and to seek advice about Jackie's role.

Athena was extremely pleased with the appointment. She knew it was the right thing to do to help Paul. As he's sure going to need the support with what she still had planned for the business.

"Fantastic news Paul," Athena began. "On Monday Jackie needs educating about your health, our business transformation project, the ideology of the business, the roles and characteristics of the team and her job description."

"I'm comfortable doing all of that, except for the job description bit," Worried Paul. "I've never had a general manager. Where do I start?"

"It's straightforward Paul." Explained Athena. "Jackie is responsible for hitting the financial targets. And to do this she needs to make sure the team hit all theirs, including their key performance indicators (KPI's)."

"Jackie is a very experienced individual and she'll know much more than you about processes, procedures, management of team and key measures."

"The best approach is to work with Jackie and let her write her own job description, once she's got to grips with the individuals and task at hand."

"Get Jackie settled in next week and then, just leave her to lead the team. But. Set up a fortnightly review meeting. To review financial and operational performance, and where you can both discuss any other issues openly."

"Come back and see me a week on Monday, as it's time for phase five."

Paul looked at Athena in amazement. He thought this woman (although amazing) was relentless. Standing, they had a hug and said their goodbyes.

Chapter 14. Finding our Way

Jackie was waiting outside when Paul arrived; "Good morning Jackie, you're early."

"Good morning Paul, "Jackie returned. "I hate being late for anything, so I usually end up arriving much too early."

"Come on in, I'll put the kettle on," smiled Paul. "Once all the team arrive, we'll pop in and see them for a few minutes, before your induction."

The team were happy to see Jackie again. They chatted for a few minutes and Jackie said her goodbyes and joined Paul in his office.

"Jackie I'm really pleased you've agreed to join us." Grinned Paul, "I want to reassure you I won't be constantly on your case, I'll let you lead freely."

"You've got masses of experience in managing teams and achieving targets. Much more than me, which is why we've brought you in."

"My only request is we have a fortnightly review meeting. To review the financial and operational performance of the business. And where we can both discuss any other issues openly without recourse."

"Thank you for confirming that Paul," smiled Jackie. "And I agree on the timing and topic of the review meetings."

"Jackie. Today I want to explain about my health, the business transformation project we're rolling out, the ideology of the business, the roles and characteristics of the team and your job description," said Paul.

"Perfect," confirmed Jackie.

Paul started from the beginning. He was honest and open about his mentoring relationship with Athena; how'd they met when he was at his lowest point and the plan they'd designed and started to implement.

Then he explained about the big move, closing the stores, losing thousands and the work they'd put in to save the business. And how on Christmas day it brought him to his knees. Which is why Jackie now finds herself involved.

"Wow!" commented Jackie, looking totally gob smacked, "That's one hell of an amazing journey. I'll try my best to lessen the troughs now I'm here."

Paul smiled, knowing exactly what Jackie meant. He went on to explain the strategy that he and Athena had mapped out.

Taking IBM's enterprise strategy, repackaging it and delivering it with honesty and transparency to SME's in affordable subscriptions. With a long-term vision to make office technology solutions affordable for all.

"There are some inherent problems in our industry, Jackie," Paul explained. "Some suppliers hoodwink customers, making it difficult to understand terms, overcharge and make it impossible to leave even if service is poor."

"Sounds similar to the financial industry Paul." Replied Jackie. "You know. People just want simple honest service. And if you can provide it, they've no reason to leave and will stick with you forever."

Paul immediately knew they'd employed the right person. Only a few short months ago, he'd sat with Steph to map out the new corporate website, and that's exactly the strapline that they'd both agreed on. It was meant to be.

Moving on. Paul explained the team structure and their characteristics. Explaining why they'd recently lost Barry. And after much debate. That Don and Harry had agreed to manage his customers and targets for his bonus.

That then brought the conversation to Jackie's job description.

Paul began; "Jackie I won't insult you, by thinking I know more about managing, achieving targets, and getting the best out of teams than you do.

"Here are the targets we need to achieve, and this is the monthly bonus I can afford to pay you for achieving them (handing Jackie a spreadsheet.)"

"I'm suggesting you take a month to assess everything and to write your own job description. We'll then have our first review meeting, where you can present your plans and recommendations for the future. Is that fair."

"Absolutely." Agreed Jackie. With that Jackie got up. Thanked Paul for his time and went to join the team in the main office.

It felt odd handing responsibility for the business to a stranger. Although Jackie felt familiar and a very safe pair of hands. Paul still felt alone.

For the rest of week, Paul reverted to bold calling and leafleting. Letting Jackie find her feet and manage the team. Hearing very little from them.

Friday came. Which was normally his review day with the team members. But this is not his responsibility anymore. So how would he fill the time?

Paul had thought for a while that he needed to work on the brand recognition of the business, to support Belinda, Don, and Harry.

The best way to do this is online. Through helpful blogs and articles. Posted on websites and social media platforms. It's a time-consuming activity and although he enjoyed writing, it's not a journey he'd been able to embark on. Until now.

Steph had got the bones of the new corporate website together and had recently launched it, as a work in progress. Once Jackie had set out her strategy, she'd work with Steph and the team to refine and finish it.

But it gave Paul a vehicle to start his brand recognition project. He'd post a blog or article once a day (after his bold calling or leafleting,) and on a Friday he'd shoot a video business book review.

Paul had been listening to business books for years whilst he walked the dog. Due to his illness he was walking the dog further and more often.

This allowed him to listen to a business book every week. So, Paul thought, why not share them with others, giving them an idea of what they're about and whether they're worth an investment in time to read.

It was Monday. Paul was intrigued by what today's meeting with Athena held. What was phase five. Had they not developed everything they could already?

Where was Athena. Paul was banging on the door and ringing the bell. Was she round the back doing that Jiu Jitsu stuff again? But there was no note on the door this time. He went round the back to see. There was no sign of her.

Paul was disappointed, he was looking forward to seeing Athena again. He'd grown fond of her and missed being together. The attraction was still strong. But it was much more than that. He had a feeling she was special.

Just as he turned to make his way back to his car, Paul heard a whirring of helicopter blades. It was getting louder, which meant closer. A large black sleek looking helicopter whooshed over the roof of the house.

Paul looked up. Athena was at the controls waving down at him. This was no humpty dumpty helicopter. It was the world's fastest. Called a Eurocopter X3 and could reach speeds of 293mph; Paul was excited, being a copter geek.

Athena hovered the monster of a machine over a large grassed area in the garden. Suddenly there was a rumble, a large round area of the grass had lowered slightly and then slide open in two parts from the centre.

Paul couldn't believe it. He thought he was in the middle of a James Bond movie. It was about time they had a female Bond he thought to himself.

The two grassed half circles fully opened, leaving a dark cavernous hole beneath. Athena slowly lowered the helicopter deep inside, the engine noise died, and the grass half circles slowly closed above with a final clang.

Athena removed her helmet, dismounted, and zoomed through the underground tunnel towards the house. Appearing through the rear doors in traditional white robes without a hair misplaced.

With a look of confusion on his face. Paul asked. "How'd you get there?"

"Get where." Replied Athena with a straight face.

"If that wasn't you in the helicopter. Who was it then?" Questioned Paul.

"What helicopter." Laughed Athena. She broke and couldn't keep the charade up for any longer.

"How've you managed to get over there though, when you landed at the bottom of the garden?" Asked a confused Paul.

"Do you want to come and see?" Athena asked.

"Sure do." Came Paul's reply. As he made his way across the garden to meet Athena at the rear doors.

Athena led Paul through the back of the house to a secret wall panel. When opened it revealed a hidden elevator. Paul looked at Athena in surprise.

They got in and Athena explained this elevator had access to the whole house through hidden shafts. And had the ability to move forwards, back and sideways, as well as up and down. Paul was mightily impressed.

Athena punched it some coordinates. The elevator lowered for a while, before zooming forward. Within seconds stopping and opening its doors.

Directly in front stood the magnificent Eurocopter X3. Paul's eyes were wild with excitement. They disembarked the elevator and stood near the copter.

"I can't believe you've got one of these Athena." Purred Paul. "It's the fastest helicopter in the world. With a top speed of 293 mph. I thought they'd only ever made one and it was in and air museum somewhere in France."

"Let's just say. Because of the type of work, I've done. I've got friends in very powerful and prominent positions," winked Athena.

"World governments still seek my advice on pending combat situations," explained Athena. "And at a moment's notice I could be needed anywhere in the world. My aim is always to seek the quickest peaceful solution."

Athena gave Paul a guided tour of the helicopter. Even letting him sit in the pilot's seat and starting the engines. Giving him a feel of what it's like to fly.

Paul was so thankful. Helicopters had fascinated him since he was a boy. He even won the opportunity to have a lesson in a small one some years back.

"Come on Paul," encouraged Athena. "Time for us to crack on. We've got much to discuss today, Including the start of phase five."

They clambered back into the elevator and zoomed towards the house. The elevator jerked left then right, before rising slowly and coming to a halt.

Athena pressed a button. The elevator door slid open and they stepped into the study. Behind them the elevator door slid shut and a bookcase (that had opened to expose the elevator) closed and hid the elevator from view.

Paul laughed to himself. Athena seemed like a mythical government agent who made Samurai swords, defeated armies, and flew helicopters. He still couldn't work out why she'd want to help a small struggling business.

Paul brewed the coffee and they sat at the table. "Tell me about Jackie's first week please Paul, "asked Athena.

"It's been a strange week." Began Paul. "Jackie's going to fit right in. After going through everything, as we'd discussed. Jackie and I agreed she'd take a month to assess things, before making any recommendations."

"That's when it got strange for me. Handing over the baton to a stranger just didn't feel right. In the end I just got on with bold calling and leafleting."

"Friday was worse. Once I'd finished catching up with paperwork, I had nothing to do."

"So, I started a brand recognition project to support sales, With the aim of positioning myself as an industry expert. Through posting blogs and articles daily and on Friday's doing a video business book review."

"I like it Paul. It's a great idea." Agreed Athena. "Business these days is all about positioning and association. Positioning yourself in this way. Will give you credibility and help build trust with prospects and existing customers."

"Thank you, Athena," smiled Paul. "Please tell me about phase five."

"We've stabilised the business again," stated Athena. "To grow though. We need to attract slightly bigger businesses than we are. To do this. It's going to take technology solutions, developed specifically for them."

"The small organisation print service is great. But a slighter bigger business needs more robust solutions, which are faster, better quality with more features, supporting multiple people using them at the same time."

"When working with the strategic boards of IBM and HP. I did much work in this area. It seems to me; this part of the industry is ready for disruption."

Paul was listening intently. "Why do you think that Athena?"

"If I'm honest." Began Athena. "I think many suppliers are dishonest. They make it complicated for the customer to understand. Their terms are always written to protect them and make it very difficult for the customer."

"Like we've done for homes and small organisations. There's a way to cut right through, with fixed priced guarantees and with simple honest service."

"Currently, suppliers hoodwink people. Initially giving them a fair price for each page printed. Whilst tying them to agreements up to five years long."

"Then, multiple times throughout the agreement they increase prices. In many cases, Customers end up paying up to double the price they started."

"When questioned, these suppliers point to their terms. Hidden deep you'll find a clause, allowing the supplier to increase prices whenever they want."

"And unhappy customers can't leave without a severe financial penalty. They usually have to settle the remaining value of the full agreement term."

"Gosh." Paul was shocked. "Is this true."

"Absolutely," claimed Athena. "It goes deeper. These suppliers also start introducing extra charges for other things hidden in the terms. Like fictitious network peripheral charges, software updates and excessive hourly rates."

"New equipment of this type is expensive. Starting around three thousand pounds. Most will lease the equipment over three or five years, rather than use working capital."

"This presents unscrupulous suppliers with another unethical opportunity, after the service and lease agreement has passed halfway, and they have increased their cost per page price a couple of times."

"The supplier goes to the customer and tells them they'll reduce the cost per page price back down to the original amount. If the customer will agree to upgrade to some new equipment."

"The customer has an existing lease. The supplier tells them they will settle it for them. But all they do, is inflate the price of the new equipment and use the extra to pay off the old lease. Tying the customer back in for years"

"In this scenario, the customer loses and is financing fresh air. The supplier wins. Sells more new equipment and gets the old equipment to sell on too."

"Don't you need to be accredited and have trained engineers to supply and maintain this type of equipment," asked Paul.

"Yes. For new equipment," confirmed Athena. "And it's a difficult market to enter. But. I'm suggesting we come from a different angle."

"Established photocopier suppliers have a constant stream of older equipment that they don't know what to do with. But we could use it to place free into our larger (small) customers who could really use this type of technology."

"There's nothing wrong with older photocopiers and digital multi-function devices. This technology is made to be repairable and will last for years."

"Unscrupulous suppliers get their customers to buy new equipment every 3 – 5 years, using the price increase strategy. Just so they can get a constant stream of new equipment sales to supplement their service business."

"The challenge is finding a supplier who's a bit more open minded. Who can see an opportunity to make money on the older equipment they acquire. Without it impacting on their own customers and installed base of copiers."

"I'm not sure how this could work Athena," questioned Paul. "Please could you explain in a little more detail."

"Sure." Replied Athena. "Plenty of organisations you currently deal with Paul, can't afford to spend thousands on this type of technology. But They could really benefit from the extra functionality it provides."

"Besides. Those requiring a higher quality finish will already have a laser printer and be spending loads of money on cartridges. Whose total cost of ownership is double or even treble that of photocopier type technology."

"I'm suggesting that we provide these customers access to this technology in a rental model, charging a fair and reasonable price for each page they print. Everything else is included. Such as the technology, cartridges and service."

"Yes. The equipment is a few years old. But there's nothing wrong with it and it'll come with a full-service package, making it fit for their purpose."

"The customer will save up to three-thousand-pound on the cost of the equipment. Gain loads of extra functionality and half their on-going costs. They'll also gain certainty and total peace of mind too, as everything's included."

"Look Paul," Athena continued. "It's like the inkjet printer packages we provide. The difference being, we can't provide it on our own, as you need access to the right equipment and the knowledge to install and fix it."

Paul looked at Athena thoughtfully. "Do you really think we can find a provider of this type of equipment, who's willing to do a deal like this."

"It might take a bit of hunting," explained Athena. "And the deal's got to be right for both parties, but yes."

"We need a supplier willing to provide and install the equipment for free, on the understanding that they get the majority share of the cost per page. Which covers the consumables, spare parts and next day service costs."

"The way I see it. The customers will be ours and we'll invoice them directly, whilst providing first line telephone support. We'll then back off any required installations, consumables and repair jobs onto the supplier."

"We'll become the supplier's customer under a plain label agreement. Our customers who sign up to the free photocopier service, will be treated as one of our own remote locations and will be managed by ourselves."

"Yes. I understand," confirmed Paul. "We act as the sales and management company owning the customer relationship. Whilst outsourcing the supply, support and maintenance of the service."

"Exactly," agreed Athena. We'll have one trading agreement with the supplier, which we'll add equipment to as we sign up more customers. But we'll have separate service agreements with each of our customers."

"Ideally," she insisted. "We'd be providing everything ourselves. But right now, we don't have the skills, resources or cash to do it."

"There's nothing wrong with providing a plain label service. if the supplier we choose, has got similar values to us and is intent on providing a great service for a fair and reasonable price. Just like we do."

"If we want to grow as an organisation and offer customers the right kind of solutions. We must move into this space now. If that means making smaller margins for the time being, that's the price we have to pay."

"I've got to be clear with you Paul. It's not just about winning the bigger customers. As our current customers grow, they'll require solutions like this too. If we can't help them, we'll lose them to suppliers who can."

"Spend the next couple of weeks scoping out some local suppliers," said Athena. "Then, we'll meet back to discuss and map something out."

On his way home, Paul remembered about a photocopier supplier some time ago. They're located in the same building as a customer Chris had delivered to, and they were interested in a working together discussion.

Paul arranged to go see them. Warren - the business owner - seemed a nice enough guy, who seemed honest and open and willing to share information.

They discussed business models and there seemed synergy, Warren didn't want to mess around with smaller desktop printer technology, and Paul doesn't have the skills and resources to provide photocopier solutions.

Paul detailed his proposal to Warren; Just as Athena had speculated. Warren had access to a steady stream of older photocopiers. Which (currently) they stripped down for either parts or for their scrap value.

Warren explained their model of selling new photocopiers every time a contract ends, and in most instances, being able to get access to the old photocopier off the leasing company. Just as Athena discussed with him.

Warren had never been able to reuse the old photocopiers in this way, because he didn't want it to slow down sales of new equipment. And was scared customers would rather keep older equipment than buy new.

Paul has presented an opportunity, where Warren can do this, without the threat to his existing customer base. Warren was keen. Between them, they mapped out the heads of terms and how the relationship would work.

Warren agreed to have it all written up and emailed through to Paul in the next couple of days. They agreed to meet again the following week.

Paul received the proposal and agreement from Warren and took it with him to meet back with Athena.

"Talk me through it, Paul," asked Athena.

"It's uncannily similar to what you said," replied Paul (Athena was smiling knowingly.) "We'll front everything, including invoicing and managing first line support calls."

"They'll provide the equipment, installation, consumables and support. And we'll make a 20% margin on the monthly printing volumes."

"Have you had a look through the agreement?" Questioned Athena.

"Yes," confirmed Paul. "Nothing unusual jumps out at me. They've insisted on an initial 12-month term on each photocopier taken, which then reverts to rolling monthly. Which is okay and we can back off to customers too."

"And a small minimum monthly billing charge to cover their layout on equipment and resources. They want the security of some money coming in if a customer doesn't print much. Again, we can back this off too."

Athena glanced over the paperwork and asked. "Did you look him in the eyes, Paul? Do you feel you can trust this person?"

"The reason I ask. The photocopier industry is notorious for being disingenuous. Photocopier companies tend to have a win / lose mentality. They always want to win, even if that means the customer loses."

"He seemed genuine enough," replied Paul. "I don't agree with his model of making customers buy new equipment. But I've no reason not to trust him."

"Let's give it a go then," smiled Athena. "But we must always be thinking, how can we become a photocopier supply and service company ourselves. As this has to happen in the future if we are to move closer to our vision."

"This is going to take some time to bed in Paul," assured Athena. "And you'll be having your first review meeting with Jackie soon, where you'll be dropping this in her lap. Let's give it six months before we meet again."

Chapter 15. The Unexpected

It was review day. Jackie entered Paul's office and sat facing him at the small meeting table.

"So. How's your first month been Jackie?" Paul questioned cheerily.

"You know what Paul," Jackie responded. "I've really enjoyed it. To be honest. I'm still a bit lost with the technology and products, but it's coming."

"You've got a good team," continued Jackie. "They just need a bit more structure, process and guidance. Don't take that the wrong way Paul. You've just been too stretched trying to do everything yourself for too long."

"Totally agree," smiled Paul. "Any observations or recommendations?"

"Don has a fantastic way with customers and sales comes very naturally to him. Although, he needs some help with his administration." Started Jackie.

"Harry's not as confident as Don and sometimes lacks a bit of oomph. He's more than capable but needs to believe in himself a little more. Certainly, something I'll be working on with him."

"Belinda just cracks on and doesn't take much managing. She's very driven."

"The rest of the team just need a bit of direction. I need to understand a little more about what they like doing and how we can help them achieve it as the business grows."

"Steph clearly loves IT stuff and designing things, that's the path we need to follow. She's done a great job on the website, which we're refining daily."

"We've had Tim training on printer installation and maintenance, which he seems to be enjoying. Chris just cracks on with things and Adele is our catch all. Great with customers and will do anything for you."

"Personally. I don't think we've got people in exactly the right seats yet. But as I start to introduce procedures and measures, we'll see what happens. Some will rise to the challenge, but others may not."

"As you know Jackie," Paul began. "We've already lost one, who was pushed way outside his comfort zone, and would not or could not change his identity. So. Don't be surprised if we lose one or two more along the way."

"It sounds like you've had an interesting month though. It's a bit early to delve into the numbers. But we'll discuss pipelines and targets next time."

"Before I go on and discuss this next topic. Is there anything else you'd like to discuss with me Jackie. Either work related or something else?"

"No Paul," confirmed Jackie. "I'm happy and got loads of good stuff to do."

"Remember during your induction." Paul started. "When I explained the business transformation journey we are undertaking, and that Athena and I are still working on strategy and will implement further phases."

"Absolutely Paul," confirmed Jackie.

"Well. It's time to implement phase five," Paul whispered a little embarrassed.

"Paul don't worry." Countered Jackie. "You've brought me in to take the management strain off you, which enables you to concentrate more of your effort on strategy. And part of my job is to make sure it gets implemented."

'Blimey!' Paul thought to himself. 'Now I've got two amazingly strong women'.

"What's phase five?" Asked Jackie.

"To keep our business customers as they grow and to attract slighter bigger organisations." Paul explained. "We need to provide printer technology solutions which fit this customer profile."

Paul went on to explain these customers need higher quality robust equipment with lots of extra features. But couldn't or wouldn't pay thousands for it. So, they had an opportunity to disrupt the market.

Explaining, another factor, is unscrupulous suppliers overcharging, tying people into long contracts, whilst making them always buy new equipment.

"I know you mentioned some of the bad practices in my induction. But I didn't realise it was that bad," exclaimed Jackie.

"Quite clearly we have an opportunity," agreed Jackie. "But without wanting to sound negative. We don't have the skills, resources or manufacturer relationships in place to support something like this."

"I completely agree," confirmed Paul.

Jackie stared at him blankly not knowing what to say next.

Paul smiled. "Phase five is about finding a partner that could provide this service for us in the background. We will carry out sales, marketing and first line support for a 20% share of the revenue."

"If we are to achieve our long-term vision, we have to move in this direction now. Using a partner as fulfillment is only a short-term solution. As we grow and become more profitable, we'll look to take it back in house."

Paul took time to explain about the new partnership and how the relationship would work: reassuring Jackie that the partner only interacts with customers when installing or repairing the photocopier technology.

"Paul, I love it!" Expressed Jackie.

"Everybody wins. Customers get feature rich technology free, just paying for what they print. Our partner makes profit out of their older photocopiers. And we make 20%, whilst keeping and being able to win bigger customers."

"Time to get started Jackie," beamed Paul. "Please can you arrange for Steph to make up some marketing materials and add it to the new website."

"Certainly." Agreed Jackie. "I'll talk with the team now and design some training to help them. Will you be incorporating this into your bold calls?"

"Most definitely." He confirmed. "As soon as Steph completes the materials, I'll include it and be handing it to the right type and size of organisation."

Five months had passed. Jackie had found her feet and was helping the team achieve some great results. The new photocopier service was flying. With thirty sign ups already. Twenty being completely new customers.

It was a Friday. Administration day. Paul was sat at his desk going through paperwork and opening mail. After reading a letter from their photocopier service partner. Paul stopped dead in his tracks. Calling Jackie in to see him.

"Jackie," quivered Paul. "I'm gob smacked."

"What's up?" replied a very concerned Jackie.

"It's our photocopier partner, they've only gone and done to us, the exact thing that we're trying to change in this industry," said a shocked Paul, whilst handing the letter to Jackie to read.

"No!" exclaimed Jackie. "I can't believe they've started putting our prices up after just 5 months."

"It's worse than that Jackie," explained Paul. "The price increase is across every photocopier that we've currently got installed."

"We can't pass this onto our customers. We offer fixed priced guarantees, with a commitment to put an end to bad practices like this."

Paul was fuming and got on the phone to Warren. The owner of their photocopier partner. "Surely Warren you've sent this out by mistake."

"No mistake at our end Paul." Came Warren's blunt reply. "We instigate two annual price rises across all our customer base. Including you too."

"So. Warren. You're telling me." Paul sought confirmation. "You're going to increase our prices twice every year across our entire base of photocopiers."

"That's correct," confirmed Warren. "If you check your terms and conditions. There's a clause which allows us to increase prices when we like."

Putting down the phone Paul felt foolish. He now understood what customers feel like when a supplier does the same thing, hoodwinking them.

"Jackie..." Paul took a deep breath. "We've been well and truly stitched up. Please don't mention this to the team. And don't stop them from selling the free photocopier service. We're going to find a way through this and win."

Paul's next call was to Athena. Explaining what had happened and asking if they could meet early, so he could seek her guidance on what to do next.

Three days later Paul was ringing Athena's bell with a letter and contracts in hand. The door opened and there stood Athena dressed as the hooded claw from a years old cartoon series called 'The Perils of Penelope Pitstop.'

It relieved the tension. Paul burst out laughing, remembering the hooded claw was always trying to trick and hoodwink Penelope. But he was also her guardian Sylvester Sneakily. It seemed very similar to Paul's situation.

Athena welcomed Paul in with a knowing smile, and went to get changed, whilst Paul brewed the coffee.

"I'm not going to say I told you so," began Athena.

"Listen," Paul countered. "I take full responsibility. I should have thoroughly checked the terms and conditions before signing. Although, I never expected them to behave in this way to a strategic partner."

"Clearly..." stated Athena. "They don't see you as a strategic partner Paul. You're just another customer and a money-making vehicle for them."

"Have you had any thoughts on what to do?" questioned Athena. "Because we need to sever this relationship. Their values clearly do not match ours."

"Belinda's husband works for Konica Minolta and I've had a chat with him, explaining our predicament," detailed Paul. "And although Teddy can't help us directly, he's put us in contact with the right people and vouched for us."

"That's a good starting point," confirmed Athena. "It's critical that you get a meeting arranged quickly and do everything possible, so they agree to take us on as a new partner."

"I've had a good check over the contract, and we have a way out. It's going to be tough. Needing you to secure the Konica Minolta partner agreement."

"To gain accreditation you will be required to have a trained engineer. So that means putting Tim through their training programme very quickly."

"Once that's happened, it gives us access to knowledge, consumables and parts. Meaning you can install and support any future photocopier sales."

"But what about sourcing the used photocopiers?" questioned Paul.

"I'm sure there are brokers selling them. It's just a matter of finding them. Once you're in the Konica club, new contacts will show themselves."

"The contract has a three-month notice period. Which gives you this time to swap all your current photocopier customers on to technology that you own. The stars need to align Paul. But it's do-able."

"Get working on the Konica relationship and get Tim on that course as fast you can. Then come back and see me," commanded Athena.

Konica came to see Paul the following week. Paul had done his homework and written a business plan. Showing how they would scale up over three-years, committing to purchasing parts and supplies directly through Konica.

They liked his plans. It also transpired they had no partner within Paul's catchment area. The last one turned out to be Paul's current free photocopier partner, who they'd let go for undisclosed reasons.

Konica gave them the green light and the partner agreement was quickly signed. Although Tim had to complete an online course before they would allow him to attend their physical accreditation gaining course.

Then a massive hand grenade exploded...

Jackie burst into Paul's office ashen faced. "Sorry. I've got some very bad news. Tim has just handed his notice in."

"Shit." Gasped Paul holding his head in his hands. "Why?"

"He's been offered his dream job." Explained Jackie. "One of his mates works for the RAC and he's tapped him up, as they're after new recruits for battery replacement work."

Tim's passion was tinkering with cars and Paul knew immediately, there was no point trying to talk him out of it. It's a job Tim just couldn't turn down.

"Well, we've got Tim for a month, and in that time, we need him to train up Adele. Adele's technically good. So should have no problem taking over the installation and maintenance work for the desktop printer packages."

"But, What about the photocopiers?" Asked Jackie.

"Let me have a think," replied Paul.

Deep down. Paul knew they had to replace Tim with someone trained on photocopiers or at least someone capable of picking it up very quickly.

These types of individuals are paid way more money than Tim was earning. And in their current financial position Paul just couldn't see a way forward.

He put a call into Athena. "We've just been dealt a severe blow. Tim's handed his notice in and will be leaving us in a month, so there's absolutely no point in him carrying on with the Konica Minolta training."

"He was due to finish the online course next week and we have the physical course booked for the week after, with no one to attend."

"If you took two weeks out. Do you think you could finish the online course and then do the physical course to gain the accreditation?" Asked Athena.

Paul hadn't thought of this and stayed silent, whilst he collected his thoughts before answering. "Erm. Yes. I don't see why not."

"Good." Replied Athena. "That solves gaining the accreditation. I suppose the next dilemma is replacing Tim."

"Agreed," confirmed Paul. "We need to replace him with either a trained engineer or someone who has similar skills and can pick it up quickly. Ideally someone with wider IT skills too, to help us in the future with other areas."

"Someone as highly skilled as this, will demand a much higher salary than what we pay Tim. And after recently taking on Jackie, our finances are stretched to the max and we can't afford any extra cash on salaries."

"Paul!" Athena called out, like he was a naughty child. "You're not thinking outside the box."

"What do you mean." Countered Paul somewhat confused.

"Bringing control of the free photocopier service in house will give us all the generated profits. When combined with Tim's salary it will release enough monthly cash for us to employ a skilled person," explained Athena.

"We don't have much time Paul. Normally I'd insist we go through a structured recruitment process, like we did to find Jackie. It's critical we find a person who has the same values as the team, to bond immediately."

"But in this case, we don't have time, and we'll need to condense the process dramatically. But I'm concerned this could lead us to make the wrong personality appointment. Have you any ideas what to do Paul?"

Paul couldn't believe it. This time Athena was asking for his help and advice.

"Well actually," stammered Paul. "You're probably not going to like it."

"Come on... Spit it out!" demanded Athena.

"One of my good friends." Athena looked at Paul and raised her thick dark eyebrows, but Paul held firm and continued. "Works as IT and systems manager for a transport company."

"Go on..." Athena gestured tentatively.

"He does much more than what his job title suggests. Installing and fixing CCTV systems for the yard and trucks. Maintains their telephone and software systems. He's their go to man for anything slightly technical."

"Technically I've no doubt Ken would be perfect. Not just to manage the photocopiers, but further down the line when we start to look at other IT related office solutions. He'd make the perfect technical manager."

"I know he's a good friend. And the rule is never employ friends or family. But Ken is different. He's got an infectious personality and is genuinely honest. He'd be a perfect fit with the team, and they will love him."

"Not just that. Customers will love him too. People naturally warm to him and feel they can trust him. I've never come across anyone quite like him. He doesn't know it. But he'd make a perfect business networker too."

"It sounds like you've already made your mind up Paul," confirmed Athena. "Personality wise Ken sounds perfect. You know my feelings on employing friends and family. But if you're sure the situation is manageable. Go for it."

"The next two weeks are going to be tough for you Paul, and it's a good job we've got Jackie to hold things together, whilst you're concentrating on achieving the Konica Minolta accreditation."

"The first thing you must do though, is to speak with Ken and see if he'd like to at least discuss the opportunity and see where it leads. Come and update me once you've got the accreditation in the bag," Athena finished.

Paul immediately called Ken, who had just started his drive home from work. "How'd you fancy having a chat about becoming our technical manager Ken," Was Paul's opening sentence.

"Not what I was expecting," admitted Ken. "But I'll call in on my way home and you can tell me more."

When Ken arrived, Paul explained the plans they had for the business. That they're building a technical division to provide market disrupting office solutions to small and medium enterprises.

"I've had you in mind as our technical manager for a while Ken," explained Paul. "You're a perfect fit for us. You're genuine, with values that align with ours. Although, the opportunity has come much earlier than I expected."

Paul went on to explain about being hoodwinked by their free photocopier supplier, becoming a Konica Minolta partner, Tim handing in his notice and the online and physical Konica training course that he'd now got to finish.

"If I'm honest Paul," began Ken, "The opportunity excites me. I'm ready for a new challenge and the change will do me good. I've been doing the same thing for years now and I'd love a chance to learn some new skills."

"Ken," Replied Paul. "That's wonderful, but I must be honest with you too. It's going to be tough. You will be pushed way out of your comfort zone. You'll also have the opportunity to build your own technical division."

"I'm excited," confirmed Ken. "But I can't give you an answer tonight. I'll have to talk it over with Deborah and sleep on it. Especially with us all being such good friends."

Ken promised to call Paul in the morning, they shook hands and went home.

It was early. Paul was out with Shadow on his morning walk and was listening to an audio book, when a call came through. It was Ken.

"You're early," Answered Paul.

"On my way to work," replied Ken. "We start early in the transport game."

"What can I do for you?" Asked Paul. Already knowing why Ken had called.

"I'll cut to the chase, Paul. I'm all in," confirmed Ken. "Deborah and I had a good discussion last night. And if we agree to keep work and social separate, she thinks it's a great opportunity and it'll make me much happier."

"As long as you're okay with that Paul, I'm going to hand my notice in today. But you'll have to work my month notice period into your plans."

"Fantastic news." Grinned Paul. "I'm over the moon. You won't regret it Ken. Don't get me wrong, it's going to be tough. But it'll be fun too."

"The timings should work out well. The next two weeks I'm on Konica Minolta training and Tim's still with us for the next month anyway."

"But it's going to be a baptism of fire when you do start. Because you and I will be out on the road for your first month, swapping over the thirty plus photocopier customers onto our own photocopier technology."

"Don't worry about me," Ken confidently replied. "I'll be doing my own online training and practicing on the Konica we have at work. You've got my word. I'll be as ready as I can be. Together with learning on the job too."

"That's the spirit," cheered Paul. "Welcome on board."

On arriving at work Paul immediately called Jackie into see him. "I'm really sorry Jackie, I've employed someone without including you in the process."

Paul explained his telephone conversation with Athena, and how things had quickly progressed with Ken. Confirming he'll be joining in a month.

"You'll love him Jackie." Assured Paul. "He's not your typical techy. He's fun and has a great way about him. He's genuine and people naturally like him."

Jackie looked at Paul a little concerned. "I'll take your word Paul. You know better than me when it comes to the technical requirements of the job. "

"He's a good guy," Promised Paul. "I've known him years, and I'd never employ family or friends. But Ken is different. I assure you. He'll immediately bond with the team and have customers eating out the palm of his hand."

With that. Jackie smiled and went to break the news to the team. Whilst Paul got himself ready for next week's online Konica training.

For the next week Paul was glued to his laptop. The training was extremely intense. It was module after module. Each one with a test at the end. Where you had to score above a certain percentage, otherwise you failed.

It was monotonous. It felt like it was never going to end. Then to Paul's surprise on Thursday evening... Congratulations you've passed popped up.

A weight was lifted, as his five-day physical course was scheduled to start on Monday.

He'd planned to drive down on Sunday evening and stop in a local Travel Lodge. Saturday though was the worst snowfall they'd had in years.

Konica's training centre is in Oldbury, about six miles west of Birmingham. Apparently one of the worst hit places with snow in the UK.

Paul couldn't afford the training to be cancelled and tentatively set off. Conditions were extremely difficult, and it took hours to arrive. The Travel Lodge car park was deep in snow. Paul hoped he'd get out in the morning.

The morning brought chaos. BMWs and Audis spinning wheels and going no-where fast. Paul drove a little Hyundai i10. Jumping behind the wheel it floated over the snow and left the expensive German cars in its wake.

The course was quite interesting. Although very long, Paul was missing his family and team. Because of the bad weather there were only four of them. Two Konica guys retraining, a nice chap from the Isle of Man and Paul.

Friday couldn't come soon enough. It'd been a long week. They had the written test to do. Paul was nervous; he'd not experienced this since school.

Four hours later, he passed in his papers to the trainer and went to the kitchen with the other guys to grab a coffee. He seemed the most nervous, but there was a lot more riding on the result for Paul.

An hour later they were called back in the room. The trainer smiled and handed out certificates. They passed! Before leaving, Paul received documentation providing access to Konica's ordering and support portals.

On the way home after speaking with his family. Paul called Jackie and the team to give them the good news. "Only the matter of giving our notice and replacing thirty something copiers now Paul." She laughed.

Monday arrived. Paul sat with Athena. She looked stunning as always. This beautiful majestic goddess like woman, was now a very close friend.

Paul still felt attraction towards Athena. But it was no longer physical. It was more like a family bond. Like how a brother loves a sister or in Athena's case (because she now looked so young) Like how a father loves his daughter.

"Congratulations on passing the training and gaining the accreditation," smiled Athena. "I can imagine those two weeks were boring and tough."

"You've hit the nail on the head," confirmed Paul. "I'm so glad it's over, definitely not my idea of fun. But it was worth it for the accreditation."

"So, tell me about Ken?" asked Athena.

"He's raring to go. Although, he's had to work a month's notice and won't be with us for another couple of weeks. "Explained Paul. "But he's already getting stuck into some training ready for the big equipment rollout."

"He knows what's coming?" questioned Athena.

"Absolutely," confirmed Paul. "He knows exactly how tough it's going to be for the pair of us in the coming month. It's one hell of a baptism of fire."

Athena smiled before looking more pensive. "It's time to give notice to the photocopier company. You better be ready for a backlash too. Although during the notice period they shouldn't contact your customers. They will."

"Looking at their track record, I'm sure they will," agreed Paul. "Jackie and I have already discussed it. Don and Harry are in the process of contacting all our affected customers, telling them the truth."

"What. That your third part support provider has done the dirty on you and started to put prices up." Questioned Athena.

"Exactly that," said Paul. "Also saying. To secure guaranteed fixed prices, we've gained our own accreditation and engineers. And we'll be contacting them shortly to replace their current equipment with our own technology."

"Paul!" Athena said sharply. "You've got two weeks to source the refurbished photocopiers you need. So, I suggest you concentrate all your efforts on this and then help Ken with the rollout."

"Give me a call to book a meeting, once you're clear," advised Athena.

Jackie and the team agreed installation slots with affected customers, developing a rollout plan for Ken and Paul to follow. The month was jammed with most days having morning and afternoon installations.

It was a tough start for Ken. They'd meet first thing. Load up. And head off to their morning installation. Stopping for coffee and a spicy chicken wrap for lunch. Before completing their afternoon job, getting back around six.

They had lots of fun too. Meeting loads of great people and learned some amazing things very quickly. At times they felt like Peter Kay and Paddy McGuinness acting out scenes from 'Max and Paddy's Road to Nowhere'.

Athena was right about their previous photocopier supplier contacting customers. They used many dirty tricks; the worst was sending letters and emails saying we'd stopped trading and they'd taken over the business.

Out of nearly forty customers, they lost one. Who'd believed the cock and bull story that had been fed to them. And ended up signing an agreement with the previous supplier. Which they were now tied to for years.

The last job was completed. Ken and Paul returned to the unit. Placing the last of the previous supplier's photocopiers inside, waiting for it to be collected. At last they were free, Ken and Paul felt elated and had a hug.

Chapter 16. Simple Honest Service

Monday arrived. Ken could finally have his induction. Paul spent an hour with Ken discussing their plans and how he can help achieve them. Before Jackie took over to go through systems, procedures, and team integration.

Later that day Jackie came to see Paul looking concerned. Popping her head round the door asking. "Have you time to talk some things through?"

Paul thought it might be about Ken and was surprised. "Come in Jackie." They both took a seat opposite each other at the meeting table.

Jackie took a deep breath. "I don't really know how to say this. But Both Belinda and Harry handed in their notice last week. Belinda on Tuesday and Harry on Friday."

Paul's head hit the floor. The elation of overcoming last month's rollout challenge, suddenly evaporated. The feeling of fear and despair in the pit of his stomach suddenly returned. "Why?" Was all he could muster.

"Unrelated different reasons," Jackie explained. "Belinda, I understand. She wants to start her own travel business from home, and it's been on her mind for a while. She's driven and wants the challenge of doing it herself."

"With Harry though, it's different. The pressure's got to him. Since I've developed processes to measure everything.

Including the types, quantity and quality of the team's activities, he's really been pushing back against them."

"If I'm honest Paul. I don't really get it. Because he's more than capable. He just doesn't want to do the things I'm asking of him, Yes, I'm pushing him out of his comfort zone. But it's the only way he'll improve himself and us."

"It seems he just doesn't want to be pushed and wants a job where he's not put under any kind of real pressure to improve. He's got an internal marketing job working for a friend of his in an existing customer of ours."

"Listen Jackie." Paul reassured. "Things like this happen when you try to change people. Some will go with it like Don, but others reach a ceiling and struggle with it. Not wanting to step too far outside of their safety bubble."

"Harry's a good guy and I'm sad he's leaving. But we need people who embrace change. Who are willing to take new things on quickly and extract the maximum benefit. Harry will end up being a good ally for us."

"I thought you'd react much worse Paul," admitted Jackie.

"Don't mistake me Jackie, "admitted Paul. "I'm sad they're both leaving. But I also understand the reasons. If you remember not too long ago, I did warn you we may lose one or two more team members on our journey."

Jackie smiled knowingly.

"The question is" Continued Paul. "What are we going to do about it?"

"I want you to let me deal with this Paul." Replied Jackie confidently. "This gives me the opportunity to reshape the team ready for the challenges ahead."

"I've already discussed things with Don and spent the weekend working out a plan of action. I want to promote Don to Sales Manager and bring in two customer service /administrators to support him."

"Don is fantastic with customers. He's just got that way about him. His weakness is administration. Which is where the two new team members come in. And they'll also have time to take over Belinda's role too."

"I know Belinda wasn't full time. But I've worked out all the numbers. And even giving Don a small increase in salary, it won't cost us anything extra."

In the past a situation like this would cause Paul to be engulfed with fear, feeling isolated and totally alone. Jackie though is calm, thinks things through and turns these situations to her and the company's advantage.

"I trust you Jackie." Confirmed Paul. "And promise not to stick my nose in and leave the recruitment and reorganisaton to you.

Paul changed the subject. "How have you and the team found Ken?"

"They already love him. It's been a laugh a minute. I admit it. You were right. He's the perfect fit and is exactly the person the team needs right now."

Jackie thanked Paul for his time and made her way back to the main office, to start the recruitment process for the new team members.

Paul called Athena and planned to meet up the following morning. But something made him not tell Athena about Belinda and Harry leaving. He felt at peace knowing that Jackie had everything under control.

Athena was kitted in figure-hugging black leathers. Paul's eyes nearly popped out of his head. She looked stunning. "Nice look," he quipped.

"I don't know what you're laughing at Paul," smiled Athena, whilst pulling out another leather jumpsuit from behind the door. "This one's for you."

"What?" Gasped Paul. "Why?"

"We're going on a day trip." Began Athena. "I've got a friend who operates a vending machine business in Paris. He reminds me of you. His model is unique. But not too dissimilar to yours and with lots of learnings too."

"You mean I get to fly in the Eurocopter X3?" grinned Paul excitedly.

"Not until you put them leathers on," instructed Athena.

Paul didn't carry off the leathers like Athena did. Maybe it was the thinning hair, slight belly bulge or generally looking a bit rough around the edges. Although for someone in his late forties, he wasn't looking too bad.

Athena slipped into the pilot's seat, whilst Paul was much less graceful and clambered his way into the co-pilots position. Athena made sure his helmet and harness was secure, before opening the grass roof and started the engines.

The Eurocopter's five blades began slowly, before speeding into a deafening roar. They raised vertically out of the ground to a safe height before Athena sent them forwards at what seemed lightning speed.

They were cruising at ten thousand feet at a speed of two hundred and fifty miles per hour. At this speed it will only take them about two hours to reach Paris. Paul was in utter amazement.

Their helmets were fitted with speakers and a mic allowing them to talk clearly with each other. Athena spoke first. "Please update me Paul."

"Certainly," confirmed Paul. "The roll out went well. You were right about the dirty tricks. They sent letters and emails saying we'd shut down and they'd taken over the business. Luckily. Only one customer believed them."

"Ken's settled in well and the team already loves him. But. Yesterday, Jackie told me both Belinda and Harry handed in their notice last week. Belinda to start a home travel business and Harry couldn't or wouldn't change."

"You don't seem that bothered Paul," quizzed Athena.

"I'm not really," Paul answered honestly. "Don't get me wrong. I like them both and sad they're leaving, but Jackie's made it clear it creates a great opportunity to change and set us up for the future. And I trust her to do it."

Athena was beaming, "Jackie's just the person you needed Paul. Everything is going to work out just fine. You mark my words."

Paris was looming in the distance. Athena manoeuvred the Eurocopter into position and landed on the roof of a tall office building near to the Louvre.

They waited for the blades to stop before sliding out onto the roof. Directly in front of them in a small glass structure stood a well-dressed man.

"Ah..." murmured Athena. "There's Jacques."

"Jacques!" shouted Athena whilst striding over. They kissed on each cheek and hugged each other like long lost friends. "It's wonderful to see you."

"You're looking as ravishing as always Athena." Jacques replied (in one of those sexy French accents). "It's been such a long time. This must be Paul."

Jacques turned to Paul. Grabbed him by the arms and kissed him on both cheeks. "Wonderful to meet you Paul. Any friend of Athena's instantly becomes a friend of mine too."

Paul loved this man. He was so friendly. "Thank you, Jacques and the same goes for me too. It's a real pleasure to meet another of Athena's friends."

"Come on. Follow me," Jacques beckoned. "I've got coffee and croissants waiting for you downstairs."

They followed Jacques into a small lift, which transported them down ten floors to Jacques headquarters. Jacques gave them a brief guided tour, introducing his team as they passed. Before showing them into his office.

It was a roomy office with a fantastic view over the Louvre's glass pyramid. At the centre of the room was a round meeting table, four chairs, a pot of fresh coffee and a mountain of croissants.

"Please sit." Beckoned Jacques, whilst pulling a couple of chairs out.

"I've known Jacques twenty years." Athena began.

"You look younger now than when we first met," winked Jacques.

Athena smiled and carried on. "When we first met, Jacques was like you Paul. Down on his luck. With a business model that didn't work anymore."

"Ain't that the truth," admitted Jacques. "I was done Paul. There was no fight left in me. Until Athena came along and worked her magic on me."

"We used to operate like all the other office vending machine suppliers. Customers would rent the machines from us, and then call us when they needed refilling or repaired, and we'd invoice them for what they'd used."

"It was a very hard and cut-throat business. You could easily lose customers because you charge two pence more for a KitKat than another supplier."

"Athena showed me a new way. It was so simple, but it was also a world away from how the rest of the industry operated."

"Together we worked out the right target market for the new service, and built a vending solution based on the number of employees located in the office it serviced. Which scaled up or down depending on numbers."

"Immediately. It transported our business into its own marketplace. Gone were the hundreds of individual small invoices and the fielding of countless calls to top up a couple of Snickers or to fill the coffee bean container."

"We moved to a subscription-based model with one fixed monthly charge, based on the number of people in the office the machine serves. If the numbers increased, or decreased, so did the monthly charge. It's fair for all.

"Another huge advantage is top up and service calls. These are now automated weekly. The customer never has to call us, and machines very rarely malfunction. As we are onsite once a week for a checkup and to refill."

"That's amazing Jacques," admitted Paul. "And although in a different industry, it's very similar to what we're building too. We call it the 'Simple Honest Service' model."

"Love that Paul," Jacques gushed. "Would you mind if I borrowed that tagline too."

"Not a problem," smiled Paul. "It fits with what you're doing here perfectly."

Athena interrupted. "There's another reason why I wanted you to meet Jacques today Paul. And that's to do with his team and how engaged they are in the financial results of the business."

"I know you're building a great team Paul, and that you treat them well, letting them make key business decisions within their field of play."

"But as they help the business become more successful, you must reward them accordingly. To show you value the work they do and to help them."

"I'm not sure I understand?" admitted Paul.

"Let me explain," interjected Jacques. "I've always had a vision to financially help the good people that helped me become successful."

"In my case. That's been creating a team who helped us re-engineer the business model into the profitable organisation it is today."

"To reward them we built a profit sharing and emergency fund program. Each month we know exactly how much money the business needs to make, to pay everything it owes. Everything above this line is shared."

"10% is distributed evenly amongst the employees as a bonus, and another 10% is placed is what we call the 'emergency fund'. Any team member can put in a reasonable request for a chuck of money from this fund."

"When I say reasonable. It might be for a deposit on a house. University fees for a child. Unforeseen car repairs or medical expenses; you get the idea."

"The key though, it's governed by the team themselves, and it takes a majority vote for the funding to be released. Which also means no one bothers bringing an unworthy claim. So, most get approved."

"Just so you're clear. Out of the remaining 80% profit. 40% goes to paying off our debts, and we've still got plenty of them. With the remaining 40% being reinvested back into the business in things to help us grow, like equipment."

"Wow." Gasped Paul. "That's truly fantastic Jacques and something I definitely want to implement when we start making some profit again."

"I'm glad I could help in some way Paul," replied Jacques. "You're welcome to come visit anytime you like. As I said earlier. Any friend of Athena's is also a friend of mine."

With that the three of them stood, kissed, and hugged. Jacques showed them back to the roof. Athena and Paul boarded the Eurocopter and headed back across the channel.

"Paul." Athena said softly. "There are some things that I now need to tell you. The time has become right."

Paul looked confused but went with it. "Okay. I'm ready."

"I'm Athena. Greek Goddess of wisdom and war, and daughter to Zeus. Formally I was a fierce and ruthless warrior, but now I protect civilised life."

If he wasn't strapped in, Paul would have fallen out of his seat. He didn't know what to say. And a long uncomfortable silence ensued.

Paul's mind was racing. Was it true? She can fight. She's beautiful and she's been getting younger every time they've met. And she's definitely wise.

"I believe you," whispered Paul. Looking behind to see if anyone else was watching. Maybe even looking to see if it was stitch up, with Ant and Dec appearing and presenting him with a Saturday Night Takeaway, Gotcha!

"It all adds up Athena. I don't know why I haven't already seen it. Maybe I didn't want to see because you were helping me so much."

"The way you dress, how beautiful you are, your youth, your fighting skills, nearly breaking my nose, making Samurai swords, your vast knowledge, the people you know and even owning and flying a Eurocopter X3!"

"But..." Paul hesitated. "I have one question?"

"Ask me anything." Athena responded.

"Why help me?" Asked Paul.

"Remember when we first met?" Athena reminisced. "When I told you that I pick people in life to help, who's values align with mine. And it's true."

"Like I said in the beginning. You're a good person Paul: honest, hardworking, with good virtues, your hearts in the right place, you just needed a little help with strategy and direction."

Paul had tears in his eyes, "how will I ever repay you Athena?"

"By making sure the business survives, becomes profitable, realises it's vision and your team shares in the success." Athena replied.

"Paul," she continued. "My work with you is complete. I can't teach you anymore. It's time for you to pick up the baton and see the job through."

"But Athena," Paul stuttered. "There's still so much work to do."

"Yes, there is Paul," agreed Athena. "But you have the knowledge and the team in place to do the rest. You don't need me. You just need to believe."

With that a lightning bolt struck the helicopter and it exploded. Paul saw nothing but white space. He thought he was dead.

But he could hear a faint call in the distance. "Paul wake up, wake up Paul."

He opened his eyes and it was Jackie shaking his shoulder. "I didn't see you get back Paul. You must be tired to fall asleep at your desk like that. How was your meeting with Athena?"

"She's gone Jackie." Paul said softly. "She thinks you; the team and I can handle things from here. On the condition we promise to realise our vision."

Chapter 17. The Surprise

Three months passed and the new team were settled and set new monthly records. Paul had just launched their own version of the profit share scheme and emergency fund initiative discussed with Jacques.

Jackie had chosen well when recruiting the two new customer service /administrators. Kathleen and Michelle were a very good fit, bonded well with the team, brought many new skills, and got the best out of Don.

Ken took Adele and Steph under his wing and the three of them formed a formidable technical services team. Each of them having many unique skills, which made them a very strong unit when they pooled it together.

Then. An unexpected parcel arrived for Paul.

It was quite long, not very wide, or high and relatively light.

Paul sat at his desk and opened it. To his surprise, inside was a Samurai sword.

But not just any Samurai sword.

The very same Katana he and Athena had made together. Now complete with a decorated handle and scabbard.

Paul got emotional. He missed Athena so much.

There was a note. It was from Athena and said:

'Paul. Please don't be sad or upset'.

'You must work with your team to achieve our vision'.

'I'll always be here watching over you'.

'And one day I'll bring a new student to learn from you'.

Acknowledgements

We can honestly tell you. It's been one hell of a ride...

And we know it's nowhere near over.

Although our journey has been very extreme. One huge thing we've learnt. Time stops for no person.

Stand still and you're actually going backwards.

You've constantly got to be looking and moving forward.

Thinking (sometimes guessing with knowledge) where your market is headed. What's the latest innovation. Could you cause disruption?

Our thanks go out to all our team members (past and present) who helped us through a tough period. And. Who are now fueling new innovations, thoughts, and ideas in our quest to realise our vision.

Finally. My door is always open.

If you wish to ask any questions about our journey, please email me at darren@mytotalofficesolutions.com or if carrier pigeon is your thing (I still do it on occasion) write me at:

MY Total Office Solutions

Unit 6 The Courtyard, Grane Road

Haslingden, Lancashire, BB4 4QN

Printed in Great Britain
by Amazon